T0278036

Hidden
ICELAND

MICHAEL CHAPMAN

INTRODUCTION

Given its modern popularity as a holiday destination, it's hard to believe that Iceland was once considered a hidden secret unto itself. And yet, *the land of ice and fire*, as it became known, was indeed under-appreciated for many years, conjuring little more than fleeting thoughts that never went beyond the superficial; free-roaming sheep, rainy days, Viking settlers and stubborn fishermen in rough woolen jumpers.

With little more than 350.000 permanent residents, this lack of foreign interest was hardly surprising. Aside from enduring the odd fishing war, financial collapse or volcanic eruption, Icelanders lived a quiet existence, far removed from the frantic routines of more powerful neighbours. There had never been the need for many visitors before, and everyone appeared settled with the fact. Some Icelanders wore their isolation as a badge of honour, holding true to the belief that their 1000-year-old language, no less their heritage, was intrinsically linked to solitude.

With the 2010 eruption of the Eyjafjallajökull stratovolcano, the public perception of Iceland began a transformative change. With incredible footage of rising smoke clouds and stunning mountain scenery broadcast into homes worldwide, prospective holiday-makers soon started dreaming of their own trip to Iceland. Mother Nature had shifted the status-quo. It was now Iceland's time in the spotlight. Things would never be the same for its people again.

Travelling by way of the Ring Road, travellers were soon privy to the likes of Reynisfjara beach, Jökulsárlón glacier lagoon, Vestrahorn Mountain and Strokkur hot spring, among countless other fascinating sites. Many of these have taken on an iconic status in the years since, yet there are still hidden attractions to be found, not just in nature, but in the towns and villages too.

While mentioning the best-known points of interest, this book strives to showcase the more obscure sites in the hope of providing options for those adventuring across Iceland. So, with that out the way, let's begin – or, as the Icelanders might say, "On with the butter!" *("Áfram með smjörið!").*

ABOUT THE AUTHOR

Michael Chapman has lived in Reykjavík, Iceland since 2016. Prior to that, he studied Film & Television Production at the University of Westminster, before working as a scuba instructor in Thailand, Cyprus and Greece.

Michael first moved to Iceland to guide tours at Silfra glacial spring in Þingvellir National Park. Instantly caught-up with Iceland's welcoming community culture, poetic language and awe-inspiring landscapes, he soon refocussed his efforts on writing and has since penned numerous blogs and articles on his newfound home.

The author thanks those whose help has been invaluable in preparing this guide. To Dettie Luyten, for approaching me with this opportunity and for your patient direction throughout. To my *kærasta*, Svanhildur Sif Halldórsdóttir; your advice has shaped this book and, with any luck, revealed your homeland for the fascinating place it is. To all my friends and family, for their passion for travel and enduring kindness, and to Kara, who I hope, one day, gets to experience this place as I do.

HOW TO USE THIS BOOK

This book is intended to help travellers get to know Iceland more intimately. While it does mention the island's better-known attractions, the focus is on sites and activities often overlooked. Entries are separated into categories rather than their geography, but readers can plan out their routes using the enclosed maps.

Most destinations in the book can be visited without a guide, though many are seasonal. Some adventure excursions – such as ice caving, glacier hiking, and surfing – will require a guided tour with an appropriate operator.

The author recommends that visitors spend enough time in Iceland to explore each region and the capital city, Reykjavík. Two weeks is the perfect amount, but guests can experience many of the country's best-known highlights in just one.

The best way to explore Iceland is by renting a vehicle and driving around the country yourself. Guided trips are also available, however, these trips often follow strict itineraries that do not allow diversions, unless you opt for a private guide. There are no rail options on the island. The author should also stress that travelling in Iceland can be dangerous. Unpredictable weather, extreme climates, low-light and wide-open spaces can all get you into trouble if you're underprepared.

Finally, don't forget to bring a camera. You're going to want it.

DISCOVER MORE ONLINE

Hidden Iceland is part of the internationally successful travel guide series called *The 500 Hidden Secrets*. The series covers over 40 destinations and includes city guides, regional guides and guides that focus on a specific theme.

Curious about the other destinations? Or looking for inspiration for your next city trip? Visit THE500HIDDENSECRETS.COM. Here you can order every guide from our online shop and find tons of interesting travel content.

Also, don't forget to follow us on Instagram or Facebook for dreamy travel photos and ideas, as well as up-to-date information. Our socials are the easiest way to get in touch with us: we love hearing from you and appreciate all feedback.

the500hiddensecrets

@500hiddensecrets   #500hiddensecrets

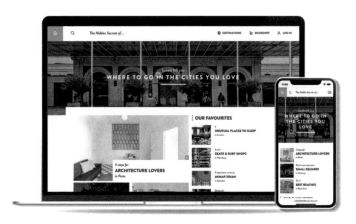

ICELAND

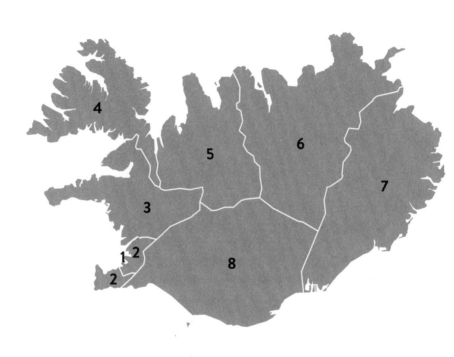

1 REYKJAVÍK

Grandi

156
192
118
28
120
Grandagarður
208 235
20
57
236
151
31
Geirsgata
258 234 186 24 266 Sæbraut
254
215
260 Lækjargata
265 214 256
23 34 203
267 189 197
210 248 268 25
53 188 202
187 246 26 224
Hringbraut 257 200 201 119
Hólavallagarður 228 190
Cemetery 48 Tjörnin 241 194 250 211
207
58 116
Hljómskála
Park Snorrabraut
96
Vatnsmýri
Suðurgata Hringbraut
Reykjavík Klambratún
City Airport

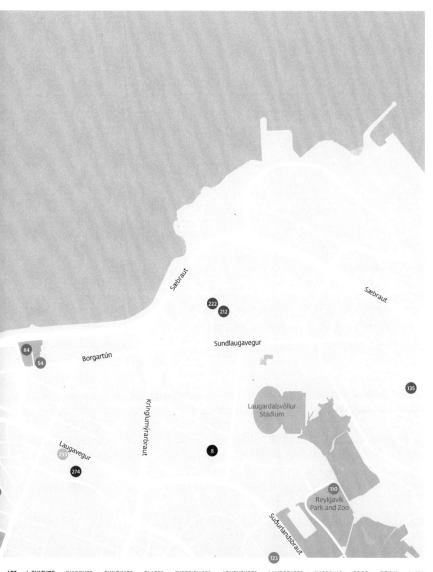

Sæbraut

222
212

Sæbraut

Sundlaugavegur

84
54

Borgartún

135

Laugardalsvöllur
Stadium

Kringlumýrarbraut

Laugavegur
293

8

274

110

Reykjavík
Park and Zoo

Suðurlandsbraut

123

2 CAPITAL REGION & REYKJANES PENINSULA

Kjalarnes

Reykjavík

Mosfellsbær

Kópavogur

Garðabær

Hafnarfjörður

Reykjanesbær

Grindavík

3 WEST

Hellissandur

Snæfellsbær

Flatey Island

kkishólmur

● Snæfellsnes Peninsula

● Reykholt

Borgarnes
●
● Borgarbyggð

●
Akranes

Ísafjörður ●
Súðavík ●
Suðureyri ●
Flateyri
Árneshreppur ●
Þingeyri ●
Hólmavík ●
Tálknafjörður ●
Bíldudalur ●
Patreksfjörður ●
Reykhólahreppur

Skagaströnd

Sauðárkrókur   Hólar

Blönduós

Vatnsnes

Varmahlíð

Hvammstangi

6 NORTHEAST

Grímsey Island

Raufarhöfn

Langanes
Peninsula

Siglufjörður

Bakkafjörður

Húsavík

Grenivík

Dalvík

Akureyri

Mývatn

7 EAST

Borgarfjörður Eystri ●

Egilsstaðir ●   ● Seyðisfjörður
                  Mjóifjörður ●
            Neskaupstaður ●
      Eskifjörður ●
      Reyðarfjörður ●

Fjarðarbraut ●
Breiðdalsvík ● ● Stöðvarfjörður

      ● Djúpivogur

Höfn í Hornafirði ●

Skaftafell
      ●

8 SOUTH & WESTMAN ISLANDS

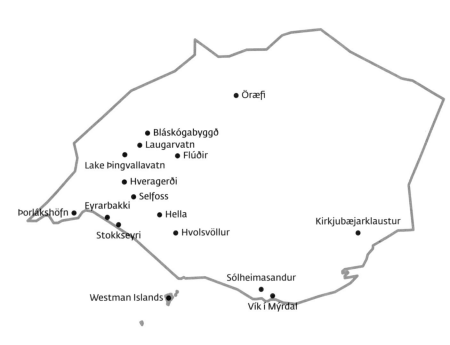

ARCTIC HENGE

ART *and* CULTURE Ⓐ

Underrated **TREASURES**

---

1 **NATURAL HISTORY MUSEUM OF KÓPAVOGUR**
Hamraborg 6
200 Kópavogur
Capital Region
+354 441 7200
natkop.kopavogur.is

Since 2002, the Natural History Museum of Kópavogur shares a building with the town's library and is within easy access from downtown Reykjavík. Its exhibitions showcase the island's diverse birdlife, mammals and fish species, and can be visited for free, making it a faultless educational stop for those rainy Icelandic days. The museum can trace its origins to Jón Bogason's private collection of 200 species of molluscs and shellfish found in Icelandic waters. His generous donation laid the groundwork for greater scientific understanding in this field, and researching aquatic ecology is still the institute's primary focus today.

2 **PETRA'S STONE COLLECTION**
Fjarðarbraut 21
755 Stöðvarfjörður
East Iceland
+354 475 8834
steinapetra.is

The result of a lifelong passion, Petra's Stone Collection showcases the diverse and fascinating geology of East Iceland. Ljósbjörg Petra María Sveinsdóttir started collecting stones in 1946, mainly from the bays of Stöðvarfjörður, though this was just one of many pursuits; ornate eggs, pens, shells, conchs and other small impedimenta all make up other collections. The recently opened Kaffi Sunnó also provides homely soups, breads and hot beverages.

3 **THE WORKSHOP**
Hjalteyri
601 Akureyri
Northeast Iceland
arnaromarsson.com

Working in collaboration with local schools, theatres and cultural societies, this concrete and industrial exhibition space is located in an old herring factory, open daily during the summer from 2 pm to 5 pm. With the first exhibition opened in 2008, The Workshop's primary goal is to increase tourism to the area, as well as further showcase the region's unique and inspiring local culture. The exhibition is operated by Gústav Geir, an interdisciplinary artist and filmmaker based in Hjalteyri.

4 **YSTAFELL TRANSPORTATION MUSEUM**
Ystafelli 3
641 Húsavík
Northeast Iceland
+354 464 3133
ystafell.is

Ystafell Transportation Museum in Húsavík is a gearhead's dream, exhibiting classic cars, repurposed tanks, giant snowmobile trucks and everything in between. Parked inside spacious indoor garages, Ystafell has laid out the history of mechanical transportation in Iceland. This collection of antique vehicles makes up the oldest and largest transportation museum in the country. The museum was founded in 1998 by Ingólfur Kristjánsson – a professional driver and motorcycle enthusiast who spent decades collecting spare parts and abandoned vehicles – and his wife Kristbjörg Jónsdóttir.

5 THE HERRING ERA MUSEUM

Snorragata 10
580 Siglufjörður
Northeast Iceland
+354 467 1604
sild.is

Considering Siglufjörður town is only an hour's drive from Akureyri, travellers in the North should do their best to make a quick visit to The Herring Era Museum. Its three distinct buildings make it the country's largest maritime museum, and each of its compelling exhibitions instil a valuable appreciation of how integral fishing was to Iceland's burgeoning economy. Among its attractions, you will see an example of a small fish processing plant, as well as a reconstructed portion of the old herring port.

Sophisticated **S C U L P T U R E S**

---

6 ARCTIC HENGE
By Road 874
675 Raufarhöfn
Northeast Iceland
+354 462 3300
northiceland.is
arctichenge.com

Located just north of Raufarhöfn, one of Iceland's most isolated villages, Arctic Henge is a fairly new structure designed to harness the midnight sun as it crowns the horizon of the Arctic Circle. Four magnificent archways represent the seasons and stand in a stoic beauty which puts one in mind of this island's ancient Norse beliefs. Each of the 72 stones is engraved with the name of the dwarves from *Völuspá (Prophecy of the Seeress)*, a poem from which this postmodern pagan edifice has taken inspiration.

7 IMAGINE PEACE TOWER BY YOKO ONO
Viðey Island
104 Reykjavík
Capital Region
imagine
peacetower.com

In dedication to the famous Beatle and late-husband of multimedia artist Yoko Ono, the Imagine Peace Tower is a shining tribute to peace, a cause widely espoused by John Lennon throughout his life. Each year, Yoko extends a welcoming invitation to Viðey Island for anyone who'd like to be present for the annual event. Through the dark winter months, the Imagine Peace Tower serves as a reminder of the enduring peace and avoidance of war that Iceland has experienced throughout its history.

8 REYKJAVÍK ART MUSEUM ÁSMUNDARSAFN

Sigtún
105 Reykjavík
Capital Region
+354 411 6430
listasafn
reykjavíkur.is

This futuristic construction was built and lived in by renowned sculptor Ásmundur Sveinsson (1893–1982). The estate now stands in dedication to the artist's work and was initially inspired by classic Mediterranean architecture. The iconic dome that sits central to the construction is surrounded by Sveinsson's sculptures, which are free to visit and appreciate for anyone passing by. Only a five-minute walk from this fascinating building is Laugardalur, one of Reykjavík's most popular parks and recreation centres.

9 EGGIN Í GLEÐIVÍK

Gleðivík Bay
765 Djúpivogur
East Iceland
djupivogur.is

Lined up decoratively along the harbourside, visitors can see the 34 giant egg sculptures of Djúpivogur, known as *Eggin í Gleðivík (The Eggs at Merry Bay)*. Each egg, designed and sculpted by visual artist Sigurður Guðmundsson, represents one of the bird species local to the area. While in Djúpivogur, make sure to visit an old fish processing factory called Bræðsla that hosts creative art exhibitions during the summer.

10 TVÍSÖNGUR

15-to-20-minute
hike from the
Brimberg fish
factory's parking
Hafnargata
710 Seyðisfjörður
East Iceland
east.is

Tvísöngur sound sculpture, designed by Berlin-based artist Lukas Kühne, is a novel stop for those passing through Seyðisfjörður. Meaning 'Twin Song', this bulbous artwork is dedicated to the island's tradition of 'five-tone harmony', a melodic oral history documented in transcriptions and recordings from the 19th and early 20th centuries. While standing inside these large concrete domes, visitors are urged to whistle and sing to bring out the different tones each edifice elicits. To experience *Tvísöngur* for yourself, walk 15 to 20 minutes down the gravel road leading away from Brimberg fish factory.

11 ORBIS ET GLOBUS

611 Grímsey Island
Northeast Iceland
+354 460 1000
akureyri.is/
grimsey-en

Translating to 'Circle and Sphere', *Orbis et Globus* is a sculpture designed by Kristinn E. Hrafnsson. The 3-metre artwork was placed on Grímsey island in 2017 and was designed to move with the changing latitude – the Arctic Circle moves forward approximately 1,5 kilometres each century. Visiting it from the harbour requires a 3-hour roundtrip, yet it has quickly become a pilgrimage of sorts for those seeking the 'sphere of the North'. Elsewhere on the island, guests can visit *The Century Stones*, which show where the edge of the Arctic Circle stopped in 1717, 1817 and 1917.

Fabulous **FESTIVALS**
and **EVENTS**

12 **FROSTBITER FILM FESTIVAL**
VARIOUS LOCATIONS
300 Akranes
West Iceland
+354 866 2053

The mutant brainchild of filmmaking husband and wife team, Lovísa Lára Halldórsdóttir and Ársæll Rafn Erlingsson, Frostbiter Horror Film Festival has been terrifying guests since November 2016. Fans of ghastly and gruesome cinema now culminate in the unassuming town of Akranes each January, hungry for the latest jump-scares provided by a range of carefully selected filmmakers. Guest speakers, pub quizzes, fancy dress and a full programme of short and feature films can all be expected. Awards are handed out for winners in special categories, including Best International Film and Best Icelandic Film.

13 **GOSLOKAHÁTÍÐ**
VARIOUS LOCATIONS
900 Westman Islands
South Iceland
visitwestman islands.com

Goslokahátíð festival takes place on the largest of the Westman Islands, Heimaey, commemorating the end of the volcanic eruption that took place there in 1973. Held each year on the first weekend of July, musicians, cultural acts and festivalgoers all descend on this picturesque isle to pitch their tents and bask in a community-driven event surrounded by pristine nature. Expect everything from large crowds to thumping beats, fancy costumes and funfair rides.

14 ALDREI FÓR ÉG SUÐUR (I NEVER WENT SOUTH)

Junction of
Ásgeirsgata and
Suðurgata streets
400 Ísafjörður
Westfjords
aldrei.is

The Aldrei fór ég suður music festival in Ísafjörður was first established by the folk-musician Mugison and his father in 2004. It is now considered a staple event on the yearly culture circuit. The entire operation is undertaken by volunteers and is free to enter for anyone willing to make the long journey north to the Westfjords. 'I Never Went South' is a reference to how some Icelandic entertainers head to Reykjavík in search of fame and glory.

15 EISTNAFLUG METAL FESTIVAL

Egilsbúð,
Egilsbraut 1
740 Neskaupstaður
East Iceland
eistnaflug.is

Scandinavia has long been known as the home of black and death metal, which makes Neskaupstaður in East Iceland an unsurprising setting for this annual congregation of leather-clad rockers. Having previously hosted some of the biggest names in the genre, this is a festival that demands any music fan's attention, though the sheer volume blaring from their speakers will likely do that anyway. The festival motto is "Don't Be A Jerk", and rightly enough, Eistnaflug has the fortunate reputation for being one of Iceland's friendliest and trouble-free festivals.

16 LUNGA ART FESTIVAL

Hafnargata 44
710 Seyðisfjörður
East Iceland
+354 866 3046
lunga.is

LungA Art Festival first came to light in 2000, dazzling Seyðisfjörður with a mixture of musical acts, entertaining workshops and creative exhibitions. Every July since has seen the festival reach new heights, with recent workshops including improvisational comedy, songwriting and dance. The festival is run by the LungA art school and is an attractive sideshow for those lucky enough to be travelling through East Iceland in the summer.

Not-to-miss

HISTORICAL MUSEUMS

17 **ICELANDIC WARTIME MUSEUM – ÍSLENSKA STRÍÐSÁRASAFNIÐ**
Heiðarvegur 37
730 Reyðarfjörður
East Iceland
+354 470 9000
en.visitfjardabyggd.is

Fearing German interest towards Iceland during WWII, Britain executed a preemptive invasion known as Operation Fork in 1941. The move would have profound effects for years to come. Industrialisation was rapidly pushed with the construction of airports, hospitals and roads, and cultural influences seeped into domestic life. Such change caused great divisions among Icelanders as how best to steer the country into a future dominated by global conflict. The Icelandic Wartime Museum in Reyðarfjörður delves into this troubled period in great detail, introducing foreign guests to a side of the war rarely seen.

18 ÁRBÆR OPEN AIR MUSEUM

Kistuhylur 4
110 Reykjavík
Capital Region
+354 411 6304
borgarsogusafn.is

If you're interested in Icelandic history, Árbær Open Air Museum is only a short distance from downtown Reykjavík. With grand wooden architecture and homes dating back to the early 19th century, this detailed visitors' attraction provides an intriguing insight into the hard realities of life here in days gone by. Árbær hosts several entertaining guided tours, which see their dedicated and theatrical staff dressing in period clothing to add further immersion. You will be able to explore actual historic buildings relocated to the site, finding them furnished with assorted artefacts, grainy black and white photographs and full information boards.

19 VIKING WORLD

Víkingabraut 1
260 Reykjanesbær
Reykjanes
Peninsula
+354 422 2000
vikingworld.is

Found amid the rocky outcrops of Reykjanes Peninsula, Viking World offers guests the chance to see a reconstructed longship, as well as countless relics that teach us more about this island's earliest ancestors. The Vikings were battle-hardened seafarers who sailed the ocean on longships in search of adventure, plunder and expansion; it is only because some chose to stop and stay in Iceland that our country exists today. The museum boasts four significant exhibitions, including 'Fate of the Gods', which explores the Viking's pagan worldview.

20 REYKJAVÍK MARITIME MUSEUM

Grandagarður 8
101 Reykjavík
Capital Region
+354 411 6340
reykjavikmuseum.is

Óðinn is the Reykjavík Maritime Museum's most prominent exhibit, a Coast Guard vessel that allows guests to discover its many cabins and impressive engine room. Óðinn played a crucial role in The Cod Wars, a dispute over fishing rights between Britain and Iceland that lasted three separate bouts from 1958 to 1976. Using the Royal Navy, Britain sought to push back on Iceland's expanded fishing zones, creating a true David vs Goliath situation. Ships rammed into one another regularly throughout the conflict, but the disparity in military might soon became an embarrassment among diplomats and, eventually, Britain backed down.

20 REYKJAVÍK MARITIME MUSEUM

QUIRKY MUSEUMS
worth a visit

21 SKRÍMSLASETRIÐ – SEA MONSTER MUSEUM
Strandgötu 7
465 Bíldudalur
Westfjords
+354 456 6666
skrimsli.is

As a fishing nation, fear of sea monsters is rife in Icelandic folklore, as testified through thousands of written accounts from local history. Such sub-aquatic terrors as the otter-like fjörulalli (Shore Laddie) and the bulbous hafmaður (Merman) are considered locals to the Westfjords region. Luckily, there is no better place to learn about such creatures than the scenic coastal village of Bíldudalur, where an entire museum is dedicated to this lore. Multimedia displays and fantastically antiquated reconstructions only add to the fantasy at Skrímslasetrið Sea Monster Museum, bringing such nasty behemoths into the imagination of the 21st century.

22 HVERSDAGSSAFN – MUSEUM OF EVERYDAY LIFE

Hafnarstræti 5
400 Ísafjörður
Westfjords
+354 770 5503
everydaylife.is

The Museum of Everyday Life boasts novelty collections of objects that at first seem mundane, but shine when curated with care and attention. Expect a blend of nostalgia and humour when looking over their displays; books, shoes and photographs all take on a new life when gazed upon with an artistic eye. There is a small cinema showcasing three short films: *Northern Lights, The Sounds from the Kitchen* and *Waiting for the Storm*, each of which examines Iceland's extraordinary society. Note that all displays are in both English and Icelandic, though there are also handy companion catalogues written in French and German, too.

23 ICELANDIC PUNK MUSEUM

Bankastræti 2
101 Reykjavík
Capital Region
+354 568 2003

Found inside a former Reykjavík public toilet, the Icelandic Punk Museum makes for a quirky stop while strolling around the city. Music blares from its speakers daily, and the graffiti-laden staircase leading below street-level promises unusual delights. Many may be unaware as to the impact punk music has made on Iceland's culture. For instance, the singer, Björk, was first a member of punk-outfit Tappi Tíkarrass, and the former mayor of Reykjavík, Jón Gnarr, accredits the British band, Crass, for his success. It should come as no surprise that the museum was opened by Sex Pistols legend, Johnny Rotton, in 2016.

24 HIÐ ÍSLENZKA REÐASAFN – PHALLOLOGICAL MUSEUM

Kalkofnsvegur 2
Hafnartorg
101 Reykjavík
Capital Region
+354 561 6663
phallus.is

The Icelandic Phallological Museum is now safely tucked away in the basement of H&M at Hafnartorg; 2020 saw it moved from its former spot exposed unimpressively on Hlemmur Square. With three times the space and a new cafe, it remains the only museum on earth dedicated to the intromittent organ. The castrated goolies of countless species are displayed, including those of harp seals, whales and foxes. There's even a metal cast of each member in the National Handball Team. The adjourning souvenir shop makes for a good laugh with its goolie-inspired merchandising, offering penis pasta, willy-warmers and Geysir-themed condoms.

Genteel GALLERIES

25 **DEAD GALLERY /
STUDIO**
Laugavegur 29
101 Reykjavík
Capital Region
dead.is

Hidden down an alley just off Laugavegur, DEAD
Gallery is the headquarters of multimedia artist
Jón Sæmundur. Diagnosed with HIV in 1994, Jón
was forced to confront the boundaries of life and
death. His exploration into this most poignant
of dualities has emerged in his iconic paintings.
His watercolours of the jet-black façade known
as *Spirit* have since been extended into vibrant
kaleidoscopic canvases that hang proudly in many
Icelandic homes. Jón has not only limited himself
to painting but also produces films, sculpture,
a clothing line and regularly performs with his
band, The Dead Skeletons.

26 **GALLERY PORT**
Laugavegur 32
101 Reykjavík
Capital Region
+354 780 2222

Art lovers can be sure they'll find the best work
Icelandic creatives have to offer at Gallery Port
which acts as both a gallery and studio. With
a rapid turnover of exhibitions, one is never quite
sure what to expect, but can always be certain
of the artworks' quality. Although Gallery Port
is located down Laugavegur shopping street,
it's housed in such a small space that blink, and
you'll miss it.

27 GERÐARSAFN KÓPAVOGUR ART MUSEUM

Hamraborg 4
200 Kópavogur
Capital Region
+354 441 7600
gerdarsafn.
kopavogur.is

First opened in 1994, Kópavogur's modern art museum hosts international and local exhibitions to complement their resident collection; works by such 20th-century artists as Barbara Árnason, Valgerður Briem and Magnús Á. Árnason. The museum was built in dedication to the artist Gerður Helgadóttir (1928-1975), an Order of the Falcon recipient known for her abstract sculptures and colourful stained glassworks, six of which can be seen displayed in Iceland churches, including nearby Kópavogskirkja. It is the only museum in Iceland dedicated to a woman, echoing its progressive philosophy towards contemporary art.

28 STÚDÍÓ ÓLAFUR ELÍASSON

AT: MARSHALL HOUSE
Grandagarður 20
101 Reykjavík
Capital Region
+354 551 3666
i8.is

The Danish-Icelandic artist Ólafur Elíasson lends his creativity to producing terrific, large-form sculptures and installations, many of which incorporate elemental themes, including light, fire, water and wind. One of his most famous and visible works is the glass and steel honeycomb architecture of Harpa Concert Hall, often lit up on the shoreline of Faxaflói Bay. Elíasson's dedicated studio can be found within the Marshall House, a former fish factory built in 1948, alongside The Living Art Museum.

Stúdíó Gerðar ↑
Gerður's Studio
Fræðslurými Workshop

Samtímalist úr safne
Contemporary art fro
Haraldur Jóns
Litrof Spectra
2017

Compelling
SHOWS *and* SPECTACLES

---

29 ICELANDIC CIRCUS – SIRKUS ÍSLANDS

VARIOUS LOCATIONS
ALL AROUND ICELAND

+354 660 0740

sirkusislands.is

Clowns and comedians, trapeze artists and stilt walkers, living statues and jugglers; all are found as part of Iceland's only travelling circus show, delighting guests throughout the summer beneath their red and white Jökla tent. Skinnsemi, an 18+ subsection of the circus, is specially orientated towards adults with acts including burlesque dancers and naked acrobatics. Hot stuff for such a cold country!

30 NEW YEAR'S EVE IN REYKJAVÍK

VARIOUS LOCATIONS

101 Reykjavík

Capital Region

+354 552 5375

visitReykjavík.is

New Year fireworks are a common tradition worldwide, but here, the spectacle is taken to a new level entirely – one that, dare it be said, stands up to titans like Sydney or New York. While not as grandiose at first, fireworks in Iceland are an all-night affair. As the clock hand approaches midnight, you'll bear witness to a dazzling display as citizens set off rockets and whizzbangs from their own backyards. Many choose to watch under Hallgrímskirkja church, though the best views are outside the city itself, preferably atop Mount Esja. The proceeds from fireworks purchases support Iceland's emergency services.

31 THE ICELANDIC SYMPHONY ORCHESTRA

AT: HARPA
CONCERT HALL

Austurbakka 2
101 Reykjavík
Capital Region
+354 528 5000
harpa.is

Those swayed by drama and power in music simply must catch a show at the glassy, iconic Harpa Concert Hall, home to the revered Icelandic Symphony Orchestra. Founded in 1950, this troupe of talented musicians have performed at such acclaimed events as the BBC Proms, plus venues such as New York's Carnegie Hall and Vienna's Musikverein. Visitors hoping for a dose of local culture can expect weekly shows performed from September to June each year.

32 ICELAND FORMULA OFFROAD

VARIOUS LOCATIONS
akis.is

Does the sound of a roaring motor tickle your adrenaline glands? Well, Iceland Formula Offroad is sure to provide you with all new levels of high-octane excitement. Each year, participants and spectators gather in the Icelandic wilderness to speed specially modified 4x4 trucks up the steepest slopes that can be found. Formula Offroad began in Iceland, and has since gone on to become known as one of the more extreme types of off-road racing one can take part in.

33 THE NIGHT OF LIGHTS / LJÓSANÓTT

240 Reykjanesbaer
Reykjanes
Peninsula
+354 421 6700
ljosanott.is

The Night of Lights festival is now a staple of the Icelandic cultural calendar, taking place on the first Saturday of September each year as a means of marking the coming of winter. Host to many different smaller events, this is a great opportunity for guests to discover sides of Icelandic life that might otherwise have been missed, whether it be music, art or theatre. At the end of the festival, a fantastic firework display brightens the night sky, illuminating the dark and craggy lava fields of Reykjanesbaer below.

Vivacious **VENUES**

34 GAMLA BÍÓ

Ingólfsstræti 2-A
101 Reykjavík
Capital Region
+354 563 4000
gamlabio.is

Elegance and sophistication are at the heart of Gamla Bíó (Old Cinema) a downtown venue built by Danish photographer Peter Petersen in 1926, with a top-floor apartment for himself (now Petersen Svítan terrace bar). As an early pioneer in film photography, the cinema showcased a wide range of films before being utilised for other purposes. In 1980, for instance, the cinema was temporarily taken over by the Icelandic Opera. Today, Gamla Bíó serves mainly as a concert hall, playing host to countless live acts. The space can also be used as a conference centre, party venue or wedding hall. If you decide to enjoy a dose of culture here, make sure to head upstairs to Petersen Svítan afterwards for panoramic views of Reykjavik's downtown.

35 THE FREEZER HOSTEL & CULTURE CENTRE

Hafnargata 16, Rif
360 Hellissandur
West Iceland
+354 833 8200
the-freezer-hostel-culture-centre.
business.site

Upon first hearing the Freezer Hostel and Culture Centre is housed in a renovated fish processing factory, one could be quick to judge unfairly. With comfortable and stylish hostel rooms decked out with trendy modern art pieces, this social venue shows just how much can be achieved in a former industrial space with a little taste and imagination. The Freezer Theatre specialises in artist-created theatre pieces performed in English, while the Culture Centre delights with its film screenings and concerts. On top of all this, the Northern Wave International Film Festival takes place here each October.

36 SALURINN

Hamraborg 6
200 Kópavogur
Capital Region
+354 441 7500
salurinn.is

Salurinn was Iceland's first concert hall designed deliberately to host live music and theatre, first opening doors in 1999. With seating available for 300 people, split between the ground level and balcony, the venue has been applauded for its modern style and fabulous acoustics, as well as for incorporating Icelandic raw materials such as spruce and stone into its design.

37 **THE GREEN HAT /
GRÆNI HATTURINN**
Hafnarstræti 96
600 Akureyri
Northeast Iceland
+354 461 4646
@graenihatturinn

The Green Hat in Akureyri is a beloved venue, attracting both local and international artists to its stage. The most popular evenings see long queues outside, but the promise of good company, refreshing drinks and awesome music makes stopping by worth the wait. The year-long performance schedule is packed with various genre acts, adding to the long list of reasons why many consider Akureyri's nightlife wildly underrated. The venue can accommodate around 200 people, with seating available on cosy round-tables close to the stage.

LANDMANNALAUGAR HILLS

DISCOVER 🔍

Famous FILM LOCATIONS

38 STAR WARS AT HJÖRLEIFSHÖFÐI

Mýrdalssandur
871 Vík í Mýrdal
South Iceland
+354 487 1480
south.is

A 3,4-kilometre looping trail in South Iceland leads to Hjörleifur's burial mound, surrounded by wildflowers and epic views of the Mýrdalssandur black sand coastline. The 221-metre (725-foot)-high inselberg Hjörleifshöfði is named after the brother of the island's first settler, Ingólfur Arnarsson. The area was used as a shooting location for the film *Rogue One: A Star Wars Story*, posing as planet Lah' mu in the film's opening scenes. Coincidentally, a nearby attraction, Gýgagjá, has been nicknamed 'Yoda Cave' because seaside erosion has carved out the cavern's entrance into this strange alien's shape, ears and all.

39 JAMES BOND AND LARA CROFT AT JÖKULSÁRLÓN LAGOON

Jökulsárlón
781 Höfn í Hornafirði
East Iceland
+354 483 4601
south.is/en

Jökulsárlón glacier lagoon provides much nostalgia for those with a keen memory of action cinema, not mentioning 90s kids in general. For not only was Pierce Brosnan's suave take on 007 pursued across this glittering ice lake in 2002's *Die Another Day*, but Jökulsárlón also backdropped for Siberia in the opening three minutes of *Lara Croft: Tomb Raider* (2001). It's easy to see why Hollywood sought to immortalise Jökulsárlón in celluloid when standing on the banks of this aquamarine lagoon.

40 GAME OF THRONES AT MÝVATN

Dimmuborgir
lava fields and
Grjótagjá cave
660 Mývatn
Northeast Iceland
+354 867 8723
visitmyvatn.is

HBO's vision of George R.R Martin's *Game of Thrones* used Iceland as a shooting location throughout its eight-season run, with the country substituting for the northernmost region in Westeros, 'Beyond The Wall'. This is a dangerous place, with Wildlings, White Walkers and vicious storms all vying to keep an adventurer down, be they Lannister, Stark or Targaryen. Visitors to Mývatn will recognise the rock formations Dimmuborgir as Mance Rayder's Wildling camp from Season 3. Also found in the area is Grjótagjá cave, where Jon Snow's intimate encounter with Ygritte took place.

41 WALTER MITTY AT STYKKISHÓLMUR

340 Stykkishólmur
West Iceland
+354 433 8100
stykkisholmur.is

Fans of Ben Stiller films will recognise Stykkishólmur town from the fantasy-drama, *The Secret Life of Walter Mitty* (2013). The town stood in for Greenland, and features in a famous scene where co-star Kristen Wiig sings a cover of David Bowie's *Space Oddity*. Her rendition of this timeless classic motivates Walter into boarding a helicopter piloted by a drunken sailor – played by the Icelandic icon, Ólafur Darri – with the two of them flying over the islands of Breiðafjörður. Other locations in Iceland were used to stand in for Afghanistan and the Himalayas, thus proving the versatility of Iceland's landscape.

42 PROMETHEUS AT DETTIFOSS

By Route 864
heading east
and route 862
heading west
661 Mývatn
Northeast Iceland
+354 462 3300
northiceland.is

Ridley Scott returned to his successful Alien franchise with *Prometheus* (2012), an epic science-fiction movie about a group of explorers who discover a clue as to mankind's origins, only to reveal themselves to terrifying interstellar entities. In the film's iconic opening scene, a humanoid alien drinks a mysterious liquid before dissolving into a nearby waterfall. This scene was shot at Dettifoss, Europe's most powerful waterfall and Northeast Iceland's most beloved natural feature. The attraction is part of the Diamond Circle sightseeing route, alongside Húsavík town and the horseshoe-shaped Ásbyrgi canyon.

Withering **(S H I P) W R E C K S**

43 ÞORGEIR GK SHIPWRECK

Austurgata 2
340 Stykkishólmur
West Iceland
+354 691 5663
kontiki.is

Þorgeir GK was a German-built first-generation steel trawler used for fishing in Icelandic waters. A storm in the 1980s tore the vessel from its anchor line, sending it crashing into the rocky shores of Landey Island, nearly turning it flat on its side. The ship has remained in its precarious position ever since. One of the best methods of appreciating this wreckage is with Kontiki Kayaking, a local company who paddles right up to the ship's rusted hull before embarking on a 1-hour voyage around the coastal islands of Breiðafjörður.

44 DC-3 PLANE WRECK

870 Sólheimasandur
South Iceland

Surrounded by the vast black emptiness of Sólheimasandur desert, the DC-3 Plane wreck makes for a peculiar artificial landmark, and yet it has become synonymous with Iceland as a travel destination. Exposed to the elements, a rusting hulk of metal alien to the landscape in which it sits, this once US Navy-owned aircraft crash-landed here on November 21st, 1973. Thankfully, all those aboard survived. In the years since, it has attracted countless curious visitors, though getting there does require a hike that should never be attempted in foggy conditions.

45 GARÐAR BA 64 SHIPWRECK

By Road 612
451 Patreksfjörður
Westfjords
+354 450 8060
westfjords.is

The ship Garðar BA 64 was built in Norway in 1912, making it the oldest steel ship ever to fish off Iceland's coast. It is stranded on a white sand beach less than 20 metres from the ocean, where its peeling maroon paint stands in perfect contrast to a backdrop of green sloping mountains. This wreck is an excellent stop for photographers seeking the ultimate Westfjords snaps.

46 FLATEY ISLAND SHIPWRECK

345 Flatey Island
West Iceland
west.is

Flatey Island boasts two prominent shipwrecks along its winding coastline. The first and most intact of these, the Gísli Magnússon SH 101, was first built in 1947, but after suffering from engine failure just outside of Stykkishólmur town, was towed to Flatey where it remains rusting to this day. Little is known of the second boat. Much of its hull now stands empty, like a ribcage wedged into the sand. Both of these wrecks make for exciting photography stops while wandering around the island.

47 HNJÓTUR MUSEUM

Örlygshöfn
451 Patreksfjörður
Westfjords
+354 456 1511
hnjotur.is

This collection of historical artefacts is dedicated to the memory of Egils Ólafsson, a Westfjords local whose legacy lies in the museum's salvaged shipwrecks, farm equipment and furnishings. This exhibition is one of the best places to learn more about the thrilling rescue efforts that took place at Látrabjarg cliffs when in 1948 the trawler Sargon came ashore in rough weather. After 70-mph (112-km/h) gale winds made a coastal rescue impossible, coastguards and farmers braved these towering precipices with rudimentary ropes and harnesses, saving six lives in total.

48 HÓLAVALLAGARÐUR CEMETERY

Suðurgata
102 Reykjavík
Capital Region
+354 585 2700
kirkjugardar.is

Hólavallagarður cemetery promises reflective insights into the previous generations that lived in Iceland. Dense with tree cover and spotted with cracked gravestones, this 19th-century cemetery is closeby to Reykjavík's Lake Tjörnin. According to folklore, Hólavallagarður sat empty for six years upon opening as it was claimed the first person buried there would forever have to act as the cemetery's groundskeeper.

48 HÓLAVALLAGARÐUR CEMETERY

49 LAUGARDÆLA- KIRKJA / BOBBY FISCHER GRAVE

Laugardælir
801 Selfoss
South Iceland

Here lies Bobby Fischer, one of the most skilled and controversial grandmasters ever to have played chess. As the 11th world champion, Fischer retired to Iceland after years spent living as an émigré. This lifestyle was a consequence of the USA having issued warrants for his arrest following an unofficial rematch against Boris Spassky in Yugoslavia in 1992, then under a UN embargo. Fischer's political views were openly bigoted by today's standard, yet, there's no denying the significant impact he made on the game. A visit to Bobby Fischer's grave in Laugardælakirkja is sure to make for a unique and contemplative experience. On site, you will find an art installation by Sigurður Hansen, who has lovingly mounted stones with iron crosses, commemorating the 111 men that lost their lives here.

50 HAUGSNES BATTLEGROUND

Blönduhlíð
560 Varmahlíð
Northwest Iceland

A pleasant open meadow fenced in by sloping hillsides, Haugsnes battlefield is a must for visiting history buffs. Iceland's only civil war, the Age of Sturlungs, took place 1220 to 1264. Clans fought for power and control after Hákon the Old of Norway decreed to extend his rule over the island. As it happens, he got his way; Icelanders would remain under Norwegian rule until 1380. The green surroundings of this abandoned farmstead staged the bloodiest battle of the conflict, though it is nothing but peaceful today. This site can be seen while walking the famed Sturlunga Trail in Skagafjörður, alongside many other historic sites.

51 **SKÁLHOLT**

Skálholt
801 Selfoss
South Iceland
+354 486 8801
skalholt.is

As an episcopal seer, Skálholt was a crucially important location in Iceland, a centre of politics and culture that lasted from 1056 to 1785. It served as the country's last Catholic bastion when bishop Jón Arason and his sons were executed here in 1550, an event that coincided with the destruction of Skálholt's first cathedral. Now rebuilt, the building features fabulous stained-glass art by sculptors Gerður Helgadóttir and Nína Tryggvadóttir. Skálholt continues to attract thousands of visitors each year with its farmstead ambience and rich history.

Memorable MONUMENTS

---

52 SKEIÐARÁ BRIDGE MONUMENT

Off Road 1
781 Skaftafell
East Iceland
south.is

At first glance, one might believe these twisted metal girders to be all that's left of some long-abandoned infrastructure. The display board will tell you, however, it's a recognised national monument, one dedicated to the destructive powers of nature. The remnants of Skeiðará Bridge were once part of the Ring Road, but after the 1996 eruption of a volcano beneath Vatnajökull glacier, meltwater cascaded across the landscape, wiping out everything in its path. At the monument, one can also see the glacier tongues Skeiðarárjökull and Svínafellsjökull in the close distance.

53 MONUMENT TO THE UNKNOWN BUREAUCRAT

Vonarstræti 3
101 Reykjavík
Capital Region

This quirky, luckless and iconic piece by Magnús Tómasson has stood on the banks of Lake Tjörnin since 1994. It shows a man carrying a briefcase, his head and torso covered by an unsculpted rock slab. The effect is as humorous as it is tragic, revealing much about the Icelandic people's attitude to hard work in the face of resistance. The artwork turns the average bureaucrat's anonymity into one of the capital city's best-known works, and it can be found just outside of Reykjavík City Hall.

54 BERLIN WALL PIECE

Borgartún
105 Reykjavík
Capital Region
visitreykjavík.is

First displayed in Reykjavík's financial district in 2015, this 4-ton displaced slab of the Berlin Wall reinforces the historical importance of nearby Höfði House, location of the 1982 Reykjavík Summit. Gifted by the New West Berlin art gallery to the Icelandic capital in celebration of 25 years of German reunification, this sculpture gives us cause to remember the physical and ideological divisions that the Berlin Wall symbolises.

55 GERMAN MEMORIAL STONE AT VÍK Í MÝRDAL

Víkurfjara Black
Sand Beach
870 Vík í Mýrdal
South Iceland
visitvik.com

Between 1898 and 1952, over 80 German trawlers were lost in Icelandic waters, with most castaways washing up on the black shorelines of the southwest coast. During this period, over 1000 seaman died, making trawling in Icelandic waters the most dangerous job in the entire German Fishery. Yet it was only due to the help and shelter provided by local Icelanders that some of these men survived. In 2002, an understated memorial was erected by the Bremershaven Naval Museum just outside Vík í Mýrdal that gives pause to consider the duties and sacrifices made here in the past.

56 BRÁKIN MONUMENT

Brákarbraut 10
310 Borgarnes
West Iceland
west.is

The Borgarnes area is the primary setting of Egil's Saga. One major character is Egil's nursemaid, Þorgerður Brák, to whom this monument has been built in remembrance. In the story, she endangers herself by saving Egil's life after his father, Skallagrímur, attempts to murder him. Rather than face his wrath, she chooses to leap to her death from a fjord. The Brákin monument stands on the cliffside where locals believe Brák jumped. The sculpture resembles a large winged wheel as it overlooks Borgarnes' bridge and bay.

57 WORLDS WITHIN A WORLD MONUMENT

Old Harbour
101 Reykjavík
Capital Region

Reykjavík is home to CCP Games, creators of the EVE Online universe that sees players take control of a single spacecraft in a galaxy plagued by interstellar empires. Over the last ten years, Iceland has become increasingly regarded as a pioneer in digital entertainment, in large part thanks to the series' enduring popularity. CCP designers even built a monument to celebrate the 10th anniversary of EVE Online titled *Worlds Within a World*. Designed by Sigurður Guðmundsson, the artwork was first unveiled in 2014, and the names of 500.000 pilots/players can be seen engraved in tiny lettering across its surface.

Surprising **S E L F I E - S T O P S**

58 SELFIE-STATION AT HALLGRÍMSKIRKJA CHURCH

Skólavörðuholti
101 Reykjavík
Capital Region
+354 510 1000
hallgrimskirkja.is

Selfies are a big deal among holidaymakers these days; it's not good enough to visit a place anymore – one needs to prove it with thousands of nearly identical self-portraits, each taken in front of a different exotic attraction. Luckily, this is a trend for which Reykjavík's Hallgrímskirkja church readily provides. The selfie-station outside its front entrance offers the perfect frame to capture your smiling mug with the city's most iconic landmark as a backdrop. With just a few clicks of the finger, you'll have your less well-travelled friends seething with jealousy. Ah, the joys of social media!

59 HVERNIG GENGUR PHONE BOOTH

Hafnargata Road
710 Seyðisfjörður
East Iceland

This isolated and rusty sculpture known as the *How's it Going? Phonebox* was designed and built by Icelandic artist Guðjón Ketilsson in dedication to the country's first telegraph cable. Set out amidst the wilderness of a large grassy knoll north of Seyðisfjörður, this sculpture is best suited to visitors looking for peculiar hidden secrets in the countryside. The *Tvísöngur* sound sculpture is also located just a short distance away.

60 FRIÐHEIMAR TOMATO FARM

Reykholti,
Bláskógabyggð
806 Selfoss
South Iceland
+354 486 8894
fridheimar.is

Friðheimar offers far more than the three breeds of organically grown tomatoes that have made them famous in Iceland. For one, they stand behind an exquisite dining experience inside a greenhouse. If you're someone who's always taking pictures of food for Instagram, you'll find that Friðheimar's range of dishes complements your feed perfectly. If you prefer selfies, the lush plant life of the greenhouse provides a refined and health-affirming backdrop. Visitors can also take a tour of the greenhouses to see firsthand how these growers manage such lush produce all-year round with the use of geothermal energy.

61 SJÁVARSMIÐJAN SEAWEED BATHS

Vesturbraut 2
380 Reykhólah-
reppur
Westfjords
+354 859 8877
sjavarsmidjan.is

The Sjávarsmiðjan Seaweed Baths make for an unmatched getaway for anyone looking to both relax and get an invigorating body boost while travelling in the Westfjords. The natural, health-giving properties of seaweed cannot be understated; rich in antioxidants, not only do seaweed baths increase the elasticity of the skin, significantly reducing the signs of ageing, but also counter skin disorders and cellulite. Besides an unmissable opportunity to post photographs of yourself getting a seaweed facial on social media, you'll feel incredibly refreshed after a visit to this comforting spa in utterly tranquil surroundings.

62 CHRISTMAS HOUSE

Sveinsbær,
Hrafnagil
601 Akureyri
Northeast Iceland
+354 463 1433
port.is

Whoever said Santa Clause comes from Lapland (or the North Pole, depending on who you ask) has quite clearly never visited his workshop in North Iceland. This fun festive attraction is great for kids, providing an entertaining and unique insight into Icelandic Christmas traditions. The adults can enjoy traditional smoked meats in joyful surroundings, as well as show kids the wishing well located on-site. A visit to this attraction will only elevate your holiday spirits more, plus offer you a colourful backdrop for future family Christmas cards.

Valorous **VIEWS**

63 LANDMANNA-LAUGAR HILLS

FJALLABAK NATURE RESERVE, HIGHLANDS

Route 26 to 208
851 Hella
South Iceland
+354 893 8407
(Landmannalaugar campsite)
south.is

Landmannalaugar (The Pools of the People) is named due to the region's abundance of steamy geothermal pools, historically used by shepherds to help keep their livestock warm during the winter. As one walks across the hiking trails of Landmannalaugar, you'll be privy to the kaleidoscopic hillsides where the rhyolite rock reflects sunlight in all manners of colour.

63 LANDMANNALAUGAR HILLS

64 DYRHÓLAEY ROCK ARCH

Off route 218
871 Vik í Mýrdal
South Iceland
+354 487 1480
south.is

A sightseeing staple, Dyrhólaey promenade is located before Reynisfjara black sand beach when travelling from the capital. Those atop this glorious elevation will have staggering views over the meadows, bird cliffs and shoreline of South Iceland, as well as be within walking distance to Dyrhólaey lighthouse. Onlookers below can marvel at the arresting rock arch that curves dramatically upward from the ocean.

65 THE SUMMIT OF MOUNT ESJA

Mógilsá, Mount
Esja parking
162 Reykjavík
Capital Region
+354 562 2500
helicopter.is

Local fitness fanatics will regularly jog or cycle up and down Mount Esja on the weekends, but casual hikers will take approximately 3,5 hours to reach the top. Even during the summer, the mountain's highest altitudes will still hold a thin, picturesque layer of snow. One exciting means of visiting Esja's peak is to book a helicopter tour, not only bestowing you with a brilliant aerial view over the multi-coloured tin rooftops of Reykjavík but also an epic means of beating hikers to the top of the trail.

66 ÞINGVELLIR NATIONAL PARK VIEWPOINT – HAKIÐ

ÞINGVELLIR
NATIONAL PARK
801 Selfoss
South Iceland
+354 482 2660
thingvellir.is

Þingvellir National Park is one of Iceland's most popular stops. Forty minutes from Reykjavík, it makes up one-third of the Golden Circle sightseeing route alongside Gullfoss waterfall and Geysir geothermal valley. Those quickly passing through might miss out on the park's visitors centre, a modern facility sat atop the Almannagjá fault. Here, Hakið viewpoint showcases the park in its entirety: Lake Þingvallavatn and its tributaries, the surrounding mountains, Þingvallakirkja Church, and Eurasia's distant tectonic plate. As one of the most beautiful and culturally significant locations in the country, no visit to Iceland is complete without having seen Þingvellir from Hakið.

67 INSIDE-LOOK AT ÞRÍHNÚKAGÍGUR VOLCANO

MEET AT: BLÁFJÖLL
PARKING LOT
Bláfjallavegur 1
203 Kópavogur
Capital Region
+354 519 5609
insidethevolcano.com

Near the capital, one can find Þríhnúkagígur, a dormant volcano that hasn't erupted for over 4000 years. By way of a cable lift, guests can descend 120 metres into the open caldera, at which point they will see just why this natural phenomenon comes so highly praised. Vibrant red, orange and purple rock faces surround you at all times, their colour and texture forever changed by the searing heat that once built up here. Getting to Þríhnúkagígur requires a 3-kilometre hike, so a moderate level of fitness is required for visiting.

68 PERLAN MUSEUM AND OBSERVATION DECK

Öskjuhlíð
105 Reykjavík
Capital Region
+354 566 9000
perlan.is

Perlan is one of Reykjavík's better-known museums, attracting guests with impressive exhibitions and an iconic dome profile. Inside is a 100-metre-long replica ice cave and a Northern Lights planetarium show, however, its observation deck is arguably the museum's greatest asset, offering 360-degree views of Iceland's colourful capital on Faxaflói Bay. If you're looking for more reasons to pay a visit, then two 230-metre ziplines were recently added to the platform, sending guests whizzing over the pine tree tops of Öskjuhlíð hill. In the summer, family visitors can also enjoy an outdoor bouncy castle and inflatable jumping platform.

Höfði

BUILDINGS

Tremendous **TURF HOUSES**

69 LAUFÁS

Laufás
616 Grenivík
Northeast Iceland
+354 895 3172
minjasafnid.is

Early settlers used up most of Iceland's timber for boats, construction and fuel, meaning their descendants had to get creative when ensuring shelter during the long winters. Thus, turf houses soon became the staple abode for both poor and affluent residents. Operated by Akureyri Museum, the turf houses of Laufás are an excellent example of an opulent residency, once a wealthy manor and vicarage capable of housing up to 30 people. During the summer, visitors can appreciate this architecture for themselves, including a small church built in 1865. The last people living at Laufás left in 1937.

70 SKAGAFJÖRÐUR HERITAGE MUSEUM

Glaumbær
560 Varmahlíð
Northwest Iceland
+354 453 6173
glaumbaer.is

Inhabited until 1947, settlement of the Glaumbær farmstead dates back as far as 874 AD. The latest additions to the 13-building property were added between 1876 and 1879, meaning guests can be sure they're visiting an attraction steeped in authentic history. Preserved and operated by the Skagafjörður Heritage Museum since 1952, Glaumbær is particularly notable for being the home of Snorri Þorfinnsson (1010-1090), considered by many to be the first European born in North America, or Vínland, as it was then known.

71 SKÓGAR MUSEUM

Skógar
861 Hvolsvöllur
South Iceland
+354 487 8845
skogasafn.is

The first turf house ever showcased at Skógar Museum was moved from its original location in 1968. It was reconstructed to showcase the iconic abodes once found across South Iceland. Since then, a further six fully furnished turf houses have been rebuilt, each highlighting how this island's ancestors lived and worked without modern amenities. Today, Skógar has split into three parts. The first is a Folk Museum, which showcases over 15.000 regional artefacts. The second is an Open-Air Museum, focussed on historic architecture, and the third, the Technical Museum, explores transport and communication in Iceland throughout the ages.

72 GRENJAÐARSTAÐUR – THE OLD FARMHOUSE

Grenjaðarstaður
641 Húsavík
Northeast Iceland
+354 464 3688
northiceland.is

Once home to regional chieftains known as Goðar, Grenjaðarstaður in North Iceland is today considered one of the nation's most famous turf houses. Home to over 1000 cultural artefacts, as well as a rectory, post office and church, Grenjaðarstaður is Iceland's biggest collection of period buildings. With their bright white paint jobs, lush rooftops and rustic wooden interiors, visiting these turf houses is akin to stepping back into the pages of history.

71. SKÓGAR MUSEUM

73 ÞVERÁ Í LAXÁRDAL

Laugar
641 Húsavík
Northeast Iceland
+354 530 2200
thjodminjasafn.is

Situated among the green lava rock of Laxárdalur Valley, the nine Þverá turf houses were built around 1849. Their dark turf rooftops are insulated with dwarf-birch, and their squat walls are composed of hyaloclastite blocks of rock and mortar, thus yielding a fascinating insight into age-old construction methods. Þverá is notable for the streams that run directly through the homes, a design that provided direct water access to its former residents without them having to step outside. These buildings have been owned by the National Museum of Iceland since 1968, and are located only 13 km from the Grenjaðarstaður turf houses.

Lonesome **LIGHTHOUSES**

74 **HAFNARNES LIGHTHOUSE**
Hafnarnes
815 Þorlákshöfn
South Iceland
+354 483 4601
south.is

On the outskirts of Þorlákshöfn town, this little white lighthouse is no longer open to visitors but still makes for a picturesque sight from the cliff side's designated viewing area. There's nothing quite like seeing this beacon of Icelandic history standing proud on the coastline as the waves break rhythmically below. Don't be surprised if there are people in the water; the lighthouse overlooks a stretch of shoreline popular for surfing. Another lighthouse of the same name can be found in East Iceland, north of Stodvarfjordur village, and is immediately recognisable from it's bright orange paint job.

75 **KNARRARÓS LIGHTHOUSE**
Knarrarósviti
801 Selfoss
South Iceland
+354 483 4601
south.is/en

Knarrarósviti lighthouse was finished in 1939 and has remained the tallest building in South Iceland since. It is another of Axel Sveinsson's designs, this time combining functionalism and art nouveau styles in his 26,2-metre structure. Still unpainted, Knarrarósviti makes for an ideal secret spot for capturing photos of the Northern Lights.

76 AKRANES LIGHTHOUSE

Breiðargata
300 Akranes
West Iceland
+354 437 2214
west.is

At the end of a romantic coastal promenade sit two lighthouses. The first, built in 1918, is a 10-metre-high concrete cuboid that has been out of use since 1947. Nine-metres taller, the second beacon was finished in 1944 and based on plans by the civil engineer, Axel Sveinsson, who also designed many other lighthouses across the island. Open to visitors, this more recent lighthouse is as famed for its views as it is for its internal acoustics, which over the years has made it a unique and sought-out performance venue.

77 ÞRÍDRANGAR LIGHTHOUSE

VISIT WITH: HELO
Mörkin 3
108 Reykjavík
Capital Region
+354 561 6100
helo.is
flyovericeland.com

Þrídrangaviti is considered one of the world's most strange and dramatic lighthouses. Situated precariously atop an extended cluster of rock pillars that rise ominously from the sea, Þrídrangaviti is rarely visited due to its sheer isolation. Work on this lighthouse began in 1938, requiring true bravery on the part of the builders; the cliff sides fall almost vertically to the frothing Atlantic waves below, making for a treacherous climb to the top. Thanks to the miracle of aviation, the lighthouse can be seen by today's travellers while flying overhead on a private helicopter tour.

78 DALATANGI LIGHTHOUSES

Dalatangi
715 Mjóifjörður
East Iceland
+354 570 1300
visitfjardabyggd.is

Built in 1895, the original lighthouse in Mjóifjörður fjord, Dalatangaviti, fell out of use in 1908 when a new yellow lighthouse was constructed metres from it. This isolated fjord is home to only 16 residents, making it the perfect destination for travellers seeking isolation in the beautiful eastern landscape. The original lighthouse was built by Otto Wathne, a Danish shipbuilder who lived and worked in nearby Seyðisfjörður. As such, it can be considered a monument of sorts to Iceland's history as a trading port for European merchants.

76 **AKRANES LIGHTHOUSE**

Captivating **CHURCHES**

79 **STAFKIRKJAN /
HEIMAEY STAVE
CHURCH**
Skansinn
900 Westman
Islands
South Iceland

Imposing. Unusual. Fantastical. All of these words could describe Heimaey Stave Church in the Westman Islands. The Norwegian government gifted the structure as a millennial celebration of Iceland's conversion to Christianity in 1000 AD. The building is a near faultless replica of the Haltdalen Stave Church that existed in Norway around 1170 AD, explaining its foreign aesthetic.

80 **SEYÐISFJARÐAR-
KIRKJA / BLUE
CHURCH**
Bjólfsgata 10
710 Seyðisfjörður
East Iceland
blaakirkjan.is

Seyðisfjörður town's most famous landmark is this historic and pale blue church, found at the end of a street painted in vibrant rainbow colours. This makes for great photograph opportunities for those visiting this remote eastern town. Seyðisfjarðarkirkja was consecrated in 1922, a result of the efforts by the Seyðisfjörður Women's Association, and is built in a traditional Norwegian timber style.

81 BÚÐAKIRKJA / BLACK CHURCH

Búðir
356 Snæfellsbær
West Iceland

With its jet-black steeple, white wooden doors and simplistic building style, Búðakirkja is a visually appealing stop on the Snæfellsnes Peninsula. Its subdued ambience stands in staggering contrast to the surrounding lava plains and mountains, creating a beautiful, yet somewhat sinister presence. The original building can trace its roots to 1703, from which time the bell and chalice remain on display.

82 FLATEY CHURCH

345 Flatey Island
West Iceland
+354 437 2214
west.is

Behind the pulpit of Flatey Church is a painting of Jesus Christ composed in the image of film director Baltasar Kormákur – no surprises then that the artist was his father, Baltasar Samper. Other pictures on the walls and ceiling detail fishermen and workers coexisting with the primal forces of nature. All of these subjects were former residents of Flatey Island. The church inside stands in obvious dissimilarity to its exterior; unassuming, bygone, with a single steeple that marks the tallest position on the island.

Renowned **RESIDENCIES**

83 SNORRI STURLUSON MANOR RUINS

Snorrastofa
311 Reykholt
West Iceland
+354 433 8000
snorrastofa.is

Archaeology has revealed much about how the poet, chieftain and historian, Snorri Sturluson, lived at his Reykholt home during medieval times. His personal geothermal pool, Snorralaug, was among the first sites in the area to be discovered and has now been reconstructed to resemble how *The Book of Settlements* first described it. While much of the site is covered with turf, including the staircase where Snorri was murdered, tours of the museum provide greater insight into this celebrated statesman's life.

84 HÖFÐI HOUSE

Borgartún 1
105 Reykjavík
Capital Region
+354 552 5375
visitreykjavik.is

Höfði House sits along the often busy Sæbraut Road, yet most visitors passing by would give little thought to its historical value. On 11-12 October 1986, the house hosted the Reykjavík Summit between US President Ronald Reagan and General Secretary of the Soviet Union, Mikhail Gorbachev. Though these talks failed to bring an end to the Cold War, historians have since claimed the progress made here was instrumental in bringing about peace between the superpowers. Other notable attractions nearby include Harpa Concert Hall and Conference Centre and the *Sun Voyager* sculpture.

85 NORWEGIAN HOUSE

Hafnargata 5
340 Stykkishólmur
West Iceland
+354 433 8114
norskahusid.is

The Norwegian House in Stykkishólmur is noteworthy as a building thanks to its jet-black paint and prominence by the harbour front. Constructed with wood sourced from Norway, the building was finished in 1832, making it the oldest two-storey home in Iceland. Today it is a local museum, as well as a great stop to buy souvenirs and sweet products from their inhouse store.

86 GLJÚFRASTEINN

271 Mosfellsbær
Capital Region
+354 586 8066
gljufrasteinn.is/
en/home

Halldór Laxness is Iceland's only Nobel Laureate, receiving the prize in literature in 1955. His home in Mosfellsbær is now a museum dedicated to his life and remains largely unchanged from when he lived there. A multimedia presentation in the museum lobby details Laxness' writing in context to upheavals in Icelandic culture at the time; the country transformed from an island of agriculture and fishing to one of the planet's most prosperous nations. Look out for the white building with the 1968 Jaguar parked outside on the way out from Reykjavík towards Þingvellir National Park.

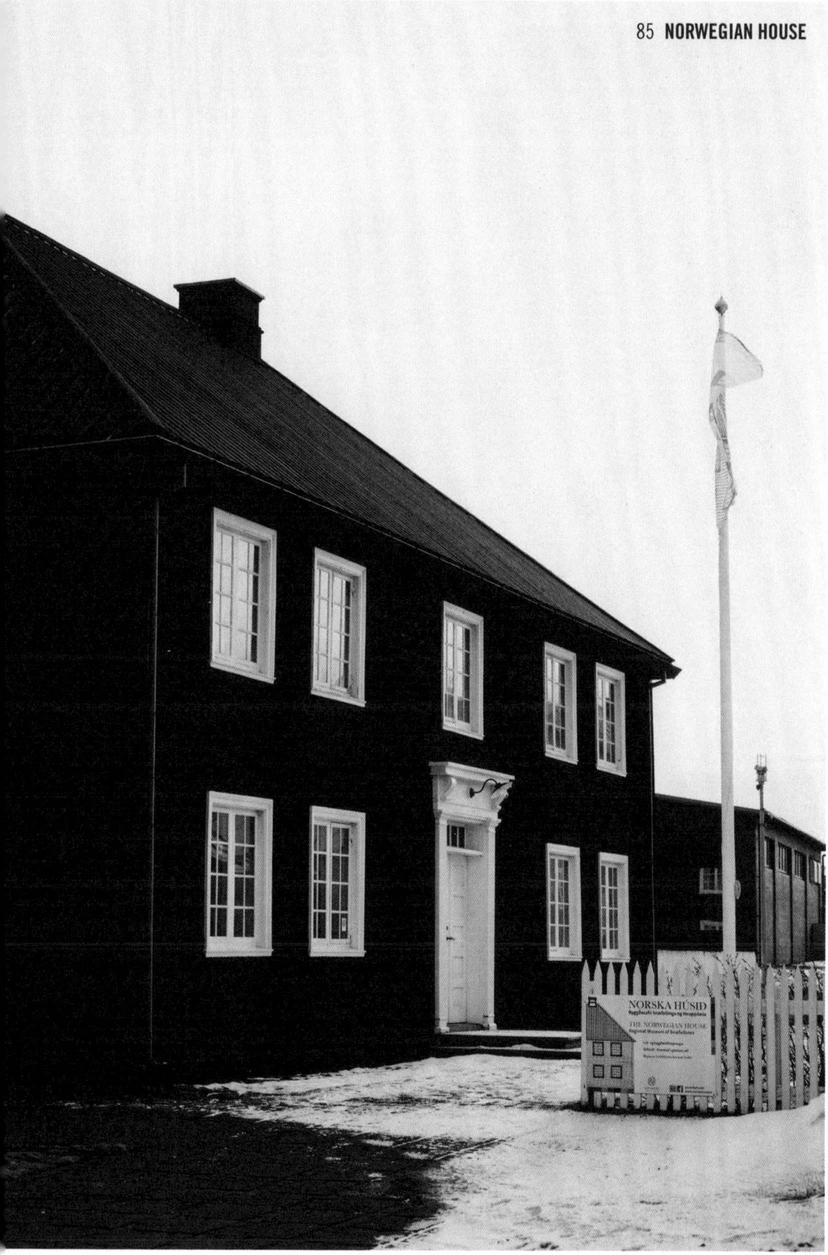
NORSKA HÚSID
THE NORWEGIAN HOUSE

AKUREYRI BOTANICAL GARDEN

PLACES 🔑

ABANDONED AREAS

worth a visit

---

87 OLD HERRING FACTORY

Djúpavík
524 Árneshreppur
Westfjords
djupavik.is

Shut down in the 1950s due to plummeting herring stock, this factory was once the largest concrete building in Iceland. Nowadays, its enormous stone chimneys stand ready to crumble, yet remain this ghost town's tallest point. A scenic waterfall cascades only metres from the abandoned site, and an old staff vessel still rests on the nearby shoreline. This juxtaposition of the stunning nature and ugly industry creates a strangely unsettling atmosphere. Ásbjörn and his wife Eva purchased the property in the 1980s. They are also responsible for operating the Krossneslaug pool and Hólmavík's Museum of Witchcraft and Sorcery. Visitors should not confuse this town's abandoned factory with the one found further north in Ingólfsfjörður, though both properties possess a similarly unsettling ambience.

88 DAGVERÐARÁ ABANDONED FARMSTEAD

Near Hellnar
356 Snæfellsbær
West Iceland

The Dagverðará farmstead is an old concrete house built in 1930. It was abandoned in the 1970s and has since remained a hollow architectural ghost on the western lava plains of the Snæfellsnes Peninsula. Today, the site is unparalleled for photographers looking to include signs of human history in their images of Snæfellsjökull glacier, which forever stands as a giant backdrop behind the building.

89 VIKING VILLAGE FILM SET

Near Viking Cafe,
Horni
781 Höfn í
Hornafirði
East Iceland
+354 478 2577
vikingcafe.is

Amidst the jutting peaks of the Stokksnes Peninsula, bewildered travellers might stumble across what appears to be the derelict ruins of a Viking Age village. However, this is an abandoned shooting location for a 2010 film that did not make it to our screens. Today, the area at the base of Mount Vestrahorn is both peaceful and dramatic, with this forgotten backlot only adding to the site's charm.

90 ABANDONED FARMSTEAD

Heiði
Langanes
Peninsula
Northeast Iceland

Along the 40-kilometre strip of Langanes (Long) Peninsula, one can find a dilapidated farmstead built in 1932 and abandoned around 20 years later. With its open window frames, dirty grey concrete, and red corrugated rooftop, this neglected property is a true prize for landscape photographers looking to blend stunning nature and ghostly history in their pictures of Iceland.

DAGVERÐARÁ ABANDONED FARMSTEAD

91 WWII RUINS

Öskjuhlíð Hill
105 Reykjavík
Capital Region

Hidden amongst the pine trees and long grass surrounding Perlan Museum are two ruined bunkers dating back to the dark days of the Second World War. In 1940, Iceland faced invasion by British forces hoping to deny Hitler a necessary strategic hold over the Atlantic Ocean. Facing out to sea, these mini-fortresses were never used in combat but still serve as a penetrating reminder of Iceland's unique situation as an occupied non-belligerent in the war. Information boards have recently been erected around the site to provide more context to these fascinating historical relics.

Gorgeous
GARDENS *and* PARKS

---

92 **AKUREYRI BOTANICAL GARDEN**

Eyrarlandsvegur
600 Akureyri
Northeast Iceland
+354 462 7487
*lystigardur.
akureyri.is*

In 1910, a group of women looking to beautify the town of Akureyri founded the Park Association. They quickly set out to make the most of a hectare of land provided to them the previous year by the local government. What followed was Iceland's first public park, extended to 3,6 hectares by 1953. In the southwest corner of the garden, visitors can look upon roughly 400 species of native flora. In total, there are over 7000 species present in the park, many of which are scientifically monitored as part of research on how plantlife can adapt in near-Arctic conditions.

93 **SKRÚÐUR BOTANICAL GARDEN**

By road 624
471 Þingeyri
Westfjords
+354 450 8060
westfjords.is

First opened on August 7th 1909, Skrúður botanical garden is one of the oldest floral collections in Iceland. Compared to the wild, dramatic landscape that surrounds it, this garden is neat and organised with lines of colourful flowers. After being restored to new glory in 1996 at the hands of dedicated residents, the park is now under the care of Ísafjörður town. Here it serves as a testament to the survival of flora in the northern climates. There is also a cafe on-site, as well as a donation box where guests can contribute to the garden's continued maintenance.

94 ELLIÐAÁRDALUR VALLEY

Elliðaárdalur
110 Reykjavík
Capital Region
+354 411 6000
visitReykjavík.is

This lush recreation area is found within a 15-minutes bus ride from downtown Reykjavík, yet it is still rarely visited by tourists. Popular among local hikers, cyclists, dog-walkers, salmon fishermen and picnickers, Elliðaárdalur Valley is also home to a stunning little waterfall known as Kermóafoss, sheltered from the city view entirely. With Kermóafoss' gentle current, multiple rocky layers, and dense surrounding tree cover, guests to Elliðaárdalur Valley will feel like they've escaped into the very heart of nature.

95 HEIÐMÖRK

Heiðmörk
110 Reykjavík
Capital Region
+354 411 6000
visitReykjavík.is

Named after Hedmark, a densely forested part of Norway, the 3200 hectares of Heiðmörk have been a conservation area since 1950. Home to over 60 wild bird species and over 150 types of wildflower, most travellers visit to see the otherworldly red pseudocraters, Rauðhólar. Heiðmörk is approximately 6 miles (10 kilometres) from Reykjavík, just a short drive southeast from the twinkling Elliðavatn Lake, and makes for a welcome break from the bustle of city life.

96 **HLJÓMSKÁLA PARK**

Hljómskálagarður
101 Reykjavík
Capital Region
+354 411 1111
reykjavik.is

Hljómskálagarðurinn (Hljömskála Park) sits on the banks of Lake Tjörnin, providing a green sanctuary within the downtown area, and closeby to some of the city's most iconic buildings. Proposals to build the park began in 1908, with the first trees planted eight years later. In 1923, a quaint white orchestra tower was built for the Reykjavík lute band, hence the park's name Hljómskálagarðurinn (Auditorium Park). A section in the southeast of the park showcases exquisite sculptures by five renowned female Icelandic artists.

92 AKUREYRI BOTANICAL GARDEN

Tantalising TOWNS
and VILLAGES

97 DALVÍK

620 Dalvíkurbyggð
Northeast Iceland
dalvikurbyggd.is

Home to around 1400 people, Dalvík (Valley town) rests on the eastern fringes of the Tröllaskagi Peninsula. This tiny fishing town boasts some attractions deemed essential to see for anyone travelling through the North. Böggvistaðafjall is favoured for its winter sports, having birthed several accomplished skiers, some of whom have competed in the Winter Olympics and other international championships. Dalvík is where visitors catch the Sæfari ferry to travel to Grímsey Island, the only Icelandic territory that falls within the Arctic Circle.

98 FLÚÐIR

845 Flúðir
South Iceland
+354 483 4601
south.is

Located near the Golden Circle sightseeing route, Flúðir is a frequent stop among visitors seeking the warm waters of The Secret Lagoon. Due to the pool's popularity, many guests overlook some of the things that make Flúðir so charming in its own right. Built atop one of the most active geothermal areas in Iceland, billowing pillars of steam are as common sight as trees and houses. The town boasts a scenic golf course, a delicious Ethiopian restaurant, and access to the mountain road Kjölur that travels between the glaciers Langjökull and Hofsjökull.

99 SEYÐISFJÖRÐUR

710 Seyðisfjörður
East Iceland
+354 472 1551
visitseydisfjordur.com

Known best for its 19th-century timber houses and its photogenic blue church, Seyðisfjörður is the first port of arrival for those travelling to Iceland from mainland Europe by way of the MS Norröna ferry. The town first became a trading centre in 1848 after local fishermen capitalised on its abundant herring stock, nicknaming it 'The Silver of the Sea'. During WWII, the town served as an allied base. Today, most visitors travel to Seyðisfjörður for either the LungA Arts Festival in July or the stunning surrounding nature: fjords, wildlife and the mountains, Strandartindur and Mount Bjólfur.

100 SIGLUFJÖRÐUR

580 Siglufjörður
Northeast Iceland
+354 462 3300
northiceland.is

As the mainland's northernmost town, Siglufjörður boasts a long and fascinating history, with much of its growth and decline throughout the years linked to the ebbing success of local fishing. What started out in 1900 as a minute hamlet founded solely for shark fishing soon became one of the country's largest towns: the undisputed capital of herring. Now home to approximately 1300 people, such amenities as a 25-metre swimming pool and a 9-hole golf course can be enjoyed in Siglufjörður, as well as acclaimed restaurants, museums and galleries.

101 PATREKSFJÖRÐUR

450 Patreksfjörður
Westfjords
+354 450 8060
westfjords.is

Patreksfjörður is home to around 660 people, and as such, is an excellent example of just how sparse of human habitation the Westfjords is. A reverend founded the town following the Christianisation of Iceland, hence the town's name, The Fjord of Saint Patrick. The most prominent attractions in the area are Dynjandi waterfall, Látrabjarg bird cliffs and the tropical-looking beach, Rauðasandur.

Unimaginable **I S L A N D S**

102 **FLATEY ISLAND**

Between
Snæfellsnes
Peninsula and
the Westfjords
345 Flatey Island
West Iceland
+354 437 2214
west.is/en

Stepping off the ferry here is like stepping back in time. Whereas elsewhere has readily adapted to the 21st century, residents of Flatey clearly missed the memo, for its scanty 18th-century architecture remains stubbornly unchanged. Settlement of this one-kilometre-wide, two-kilometre-long island dates back far further than this smattering of homes. A now non-existent monastery was established there in 1172 AD, and up until 1777, the island was considered one of the more crucial cultural and trading hubs. Visitors to this quaint island can expect flat terrain, oceanwide views and spectacular seabird colonies in summer.

103 **HEIMAEY ISLAND**

Vestmannaeyjar
Archipelago
900 Westman
Islands
South Iceland
*visitwestman
islands.com*

Heimaey is the largest island in the Vestmannaeyjar archipelago, and evidence dates initial settlement to approximately 800 AD. The Sagas claim it was first inhabited by runaway Irish slaves who were killed for vengeance by Iceland's first citizen, Ingólfur Arnarson. In 1627, the island was attacked by Ottoman pirate ships, and many islanders were taken as slaves. The island's most notable event occurred in January 1973 when the island's volcano, Eldfell, erupted. Mass evacuations took place, and the lava flow was thankfully diverted. Today, the island is home to approximately 4500 people and, in the summer, around eight million puffins.

104 DRANGEY ISLAND

Skagafjörður
550 Sauðárkrókur
Northwest Iceland
+354 821 0090 /
+354 821 0091
drangey.net

This island off northern Skagafjörður is the last remnant of a 700.000-year-old volcano. It rises from the ocean dramatically with its steep cliffs, home to gannets, kittiwakes and puffins. The island is first mentioned as a refuge for the protagonist of Grettis Saga, who fled here as early as 1031 AD, trusting the cliffs would be impassable to his pursuers. In more recent times, residents of the northern mainland have considered Drangey a harbinger of spring, sailing out to the island at the beginning of each season to collect meat, eggs and fish.

105 GRÍMSEY ISLAND

611 Grímsey Island
Northeast Iceland
+354 460 1000
akureyri.is/
grimsey-en

Home to around 60 people, Grímsey is the one place in the country that can be counted as lying within the boundary lines of the Arctic Circle. The island's one settlement, Sandvík, has historically been tied to the fertile fishing grounds, but in recent years has diversified to include guesthouses, cafes and a recently renovated harbour. The island's church was built in 1867 from driftwood and now holds a century-old painting known to be an imitation of the works of Leonardo Da Vinci. Getting to Grimsey can be achieved two ways; either by flight from Akureyri or by ferry.

EXPERIENCES ⚡

Exhilarating **ESCAPADES**

106 PARAGLIDING SOUTH COAST

Suðurvíkurvegur 5
870 Vík í Mýrdal
South Iceland
+354 698 8890
trueadventure.is

When driving along Iceland's south coast, visitors often note how much of it is lined with ancient sea cliffs. There is no more adventurous activity than leaping from one of these precipices nestled in the harness of a qualified paragliding instructor. Soaring and swooping over the green meadows of the South will bring you one step closer to feeling like an eagle (or puffin, in this case), so should certainly not be overlooked by adrenaline junkies looking for their next fix.

107 SCUBA DIVING IN DAVÍÐSGJÁ

LAKE ÞINGVALLAVATN
South Iceland
+354 578 6200
dive.is

Considered the big brother of Silfra spring, Davíðsgjá (David's Crack) is an underwater canyon that lies in the murky depths of Lake Þingvallavatn. It is advised that scuba divers visit Silfra first; Davíðsgjá is deeper, darker, and notably more dramatic, revealing a side of this country's landscape rarely seen, while also providing a little challenge for experienced divers. Unlike Silfra, scuba diving in Davíðsgjá offers the chance to see Arctic Char and many other fish species swimming in their natural habitat.

108 THE FLYING BUGGY – OVER THE CAPITAL

Meðalholt 19
105 Reykjavík
Capital Region
+354 780 6766
happyworld.is

Take to the skies in a small and specially designed flying buggy! These exciting and intimate flights of fancy often fall to the wayside in lieu of other tours, which is a shame given how exhilarating and memorable they prove to be. These micro aircraft are a heavenly means for looking down on the colourful tin rooftops of the capital city, as well as providing a level of control that is rarely granted when partaking in such extreme aerial activities. High in the sky, you'll be privy to other phenomenal panoramas, with the Atlantic coastline, mountains and lava fields only a wingtip away.

109 WHALE WATCHING

Hafnarstétt 11
640 Húsavík
Northeast Iceland
+354 464 7272
northsailing.is

Whale watching is one of Iceland's most popular activities, often undertaken on large renovated vessels. Seeing these enormous and majestic creatures with North Sailing is quite another thing entirely, as guests will board a traditional Icelandic schooner to embark from the fjords of Northeast Iceland. Húsavík is commonly referred to as the whale watching capital of Europe thanks to the breadth of species its coastal feeding grounds attract. Over 20 cetacean species call Icelandic waters home, including blue whales, minke whales, humpbacks and orcas.

Fantastic **ANIMAL FARMS**

110 HÚSDÝRA-GARÐURINN PARK & ZOO

Múlavegur 2
104 Reykjavík
Capital Region
+354 411 5900
mu.is

Húsdýragarðurinn Park & Zoo (otherwise known as Reykjavík Park & Zoo) is a wonderful spot to see Icelandic domestic animals, not to mention the handful of exotic species from elsewhere. Icelandic horses, pigs and goats are all permanent residents, and seals and minks only add to the joy and surprise of spending an afternoon here. Some rides in the children's play area are open only during the summer, though the zoo's restaurant is available all year round.

111 SLAKKI ANIMAL PARK

Vesturbyggð 10-A
801 Selfoss
South Iceland
+354 849 0661

While primarily a petting zoo, Slakki Animal Park in South Iceland also offers such fun activities as mini-golf and a children's playground. On the furrier side of things, expect animals such as puppies, kittens, rabbits, parrots and pigs during your visit. Those unable to visit the Arctic Fox Centre in Súðavík will be happy to know that these creatures can also be seen at Slakki Animal Park. This rural attraction particularly caters to children, making this a must-visit for travelling families in between sightseeing stops.

112 DALADÝRÐ PETTING ZOO

Brúnagerði
607 Akureyri
Northeast Iceland
+354 863 3112
daladyrd.is

Daladýrð offers much the same as other domestic animal parks in Iceland, though sets itself apart with its pleasant rural surroundings, putting one in mind of the large barns and horse stables of the American Wild West. It is an excellent place to see a unique breed of Icelandic sheep called Leader-wethers, whose curious personalities are more like dogs than their fellow woollybacks. Leader-wethers are even said to be able to predict weather changes, making them a true novelty for visitors. Daladýrð is a 25-minute drive from Akureyri, situated on Brúnagerði farm in the densely forested Fnjóskadalur Valley.

113 HÓLMUR FARM

Vesturbraut 6
780 Höfn í
Hornafirði
East Iceland
+354 478 2063
holmurinn.is

Married-couple Guðrún Guðmundsdóttir and Magnús Guðjónsson opened this farm-zoo after renovations to the original 1920 farmstead, which included adding a spacious cafe and restaurant in the former cow house. The domestic animals here are some of the purest bred in the world thanks to their long isolation and avoidance of outside genetic influence. Overnight guests during the winter are free to help out feeding the sheep, horses and cows, adding further reason to visit when travelling around East Iceland.

114 KAFFI KÚ

Garður
605 Akureyri
Northeast Iceland
+354 867 3826
kaffiku.is

Kaffi Kú is situated in the loft of a cow barn, allowing guests to look down through glass panels on the cattle as they enjoy any of the cafe's tasty dishes. After your meal, you are encouraged to experience the daily operations of the farm. It is quickly apparent these animals are well cared for; each cow is routinely massaged and even given a mattress on which to lie. If you're hoping to experience an authentic farm-to-table meal, this family-run establishment in the north cannot be overlooked.

115 SÓLVANGUR ICELANDIC HORSE CENTRE

Sólvangur
801 Selfoss
South Iceland
+354 899 7792
icelandichorse center.is

With a small yet muscular stature and recognisable loyalty, curiosity and intelligence, the Icelandic horse is a pure pedigree. Sólvangur is a traditional horse-breeding farm in South Iceland and one of the best locations to meet and ride these splendid animals. Riding tours are divided by skill level, while the stable visits are privately booked and personally led by an experienced and informative guide. The centre also boasts a quaint cafe built into a renovated stable and a lovely souvenir shop, perfect for those equestrians looking to remember their experience for years to come.

114 **KAFFI KÚ**

Iconic **I N D O O R S**

116 **SUNDHÖLLIN POOL**

Barónsstígur 45-A
101 Reykjavík
Capital Region
+354 411 5350
reykjavik.is

Sundhöllin is the oldest public baths in Reykjavík, opened first to city residents in 1937. Besides the hot tubs, there is both a 25-metre indoor and outdoor pool for guests to enjoy. The indoor pool comes complete with two springboards; jumping off the highest one is considered something of a right of passage for young Reykjavikings. Recent renovations saw improvements to the facility, adding an invigorating ice bath, tanning beds and a balcony sauna. The building was designed by state architect, Guðjón Samúelsson, also responsible for Hallgrímskirkja church and many other of the city's most recognisable buildings.

117 **BOGFIMISETRIÐ / ARCHERY CENTRE**

Dugguvogur 2
104 Reykjavík
Capital Region
+354 571 9330
bogfimisetrid.is

Those looking to test how they might combatively fair in the Viking Age would do well to visit Reyjavík's Archery Centre, an institution that keeps the primal art of warfare and medieval prowess alive and well. Any guest to Bogfimisetrið is sure to get a handle on how this island's ancient warriors once battled for land, love and prowess.

118 FLYOVER ICELAND

Fiskislóð 43
101 Reykjavík
Capital Region
+354 527 6700
flyovericeland.com

Reminiscent of Soarin', a flight simulator at Disney's Epcot Centre, FlyOver Iceland brings the beauty and drama of this country's nature to those staying in the city. Located in Grandi district, a giant 20-metre wraparound screen showcases glacier lagoons, mountains and erupting hot springs, paired with naturally infused scents, wind simulation and motion. All of this culminates in an experience that mirrors floating over Iceland like a bird. The two cinematic flights are led by a friendly troll guide named Sú Vitra and provide the best means of seeing Iceland for those limited to only a few days in Reykjavík.

119 REYKJAVÍK ESCAPE

Borgartún 6
105 Reykjavík
Capital Region
+354 546 0100
reykjavíkescape.com

With the ever-rising popularity of Escape Rooms, it was only a matter of time until such an establishment opened in Reykjavík. These interactive puzzles are designed for parties of four or more to test teamwork and logic, with only the smartest and most diligent participants managing to make it out of each room under the specified time. Found on Borgartún, the capital's one-street financial district, Reykjavík Escape boasts eight different experiences, themes like Hangover, The Mafia and Prison Break. On a rainy day in Reykjavík, can you overcome the odds and make it out a winner?

KIDS' *capers*

120 WHALES OF ICELAND

Fiskislóð 23-25
101 Reykjavík
Capital Region
+354 571 0077
whalesoficeland.is

This educational exhibit brings Iceland's giant sea creatures to youngsters with its life-sized models and immersive digital presentations. Children will be able to walk right up to the grandiose replicas of such majestic mammals as belugas and pilot whales. Whales of Iceland works closely with the Marine Research Institute of Iceland to track these animals' movements as they swim around the coast, a journey that can be followed by visitors at interactive stations. Kids under seven years old can visit for free, and a downloadable, multilingual app can be listened to while moving from one exhibition to the next.

121 SOUTH COAST ZIP LINE

MEETING POINT:
NORDUR VIK
870 Vík í Mýrdal
South Iceland
+354 698 8890
trueadventure.is

True Adventure focusses on paragliding, citing Iceland's picturesque South Coast among the best locations worldwide for it. Understandably, such high-flying action is not for everybody, but for those who'd like a taste of what soaring like a bird feels like, there are two ziplines – fun for the whole family. Whizzing over the stunning scenery of Grafargil (Grave Canyon), waterfalls and mossy cliff sides, you'll thank yourself for choosing to experience the south in a unique and novel way.

122 THE KJARNASKÓGUR WOODS

Kjarnavegur
601 Akureyri
Northeast Iceland
+354 462 4047
kjarnaskogur.is

The Kjarnaskógur Woods are the result of the reforestation efforts that began in 1953 with the planting of birch and larch trees. This has expanded to over 200 species in the half-century since. Today, the Kjarnaskógur Woods are considered among the most popular recreation areas in Akureyri. The region also boasts a 7-kilometre walking path, a 10-kilometre mountain bike trail, two playgrounds, a volleyball court, Hamrar campsite and birdwatching shelters. There are also picnic areas and BBQ facilities open to summer visitors.

123 KLIFURHÚSIÐ / REYKJAVÍK CLIMBING GYM

Ármúli 23
108 Reykjavík
Capital Region
+354 553 9455
klifurhusid.is

Though mainly a bouldering gym, Klifurhúsið also provides a small sports climbing wall, keeping itself open to varying skill sets. This makes it the perfect indoor activity for both active kids and parents looking to keep up with their fitness. All you need to do is come dressed in comfortable gear and a quality pair of shoes.

124 BERJAMÓ / BERRY PICKING

NEAR: HAFRAVATN LAKE
271 Mosfellsbær
Capital Region

Berjamó, Icelandic for berry-picking, takes place in the late summer, early autumn, and provides a fabulous opportunity to experience the tranquillity of Iceland's nature while putting your hands to good work. Picking berries in the wilderness means you will be away from all signs of human life, left free to enjoy the birdsong, gentle breeze and open green surroundings without any disturbance. Thanks to the ethereal cleanliness of Iceland's air and nature, berries are fresh to eat while picking, so be sure to taste-test.

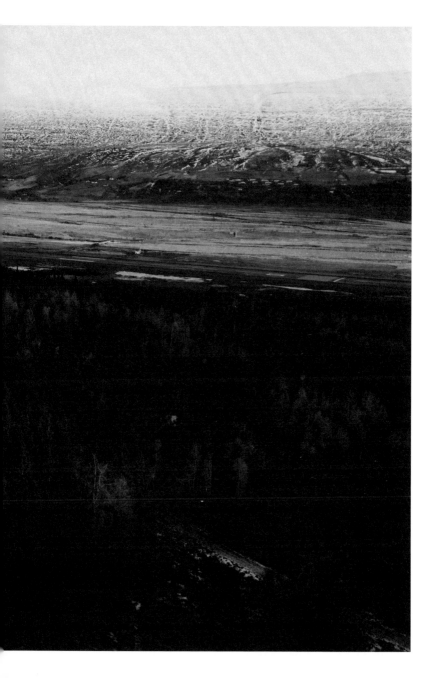

SECRET LAGOON

ADVENTURES 🐾

Bathe in glorious
GEOTHERMAL POOLS

125 GUÐLAUG BATHS

Langisandur
300 Akranes
West Iceland
+354 833 7736
akranes.is

Visiting the town of Akranes is a pure pleasure when done right. One great free attraction is Guðlaug, the local baths, situated on the banks of the town's sandy shoreline. Heated to around 39°C (102°F), guests love to warm themselves in two luxurious pools before cooling down in the frigid waters of the ocean, only a quick stroll away. On sunny days, bathers can enjoy staggering views over Faxaflói Bay, even making out the spired skyline of Reykjavík.

126 VÖK BATHS

Vök by
Urriðavatn Lake
701 Egilsstaðir
East Iceland
+354 470 9500
vokbaths.is

First opened in summer 2019, Vök Baths are built atop the stunning Lake Urriðavatn, five kilometres west of Egilsstaðir. Its geothermal pools are constructed seamlessly into the waterbody; this gives bathers the impression they are submerged in the lake itself. Other welcome facilities include an on-site sauna, in-pool bar, tearoom and their restaurant, Soups & Bistro.

127 KRAUMA

Deildartunguhver
320 Reykholt
West Iceland
+354 555 6066
krauma.is

Krauma spa is heated by Europe's most powerful hot spring, Deildartunguhver, found only metres from the elegant and modern facilities provided at Krauma. This complex is far, far smaller than the likes of the Blue Lagoon or Mývatn Nature Baths, making it something of a treasure for bathers who dislike the crowds. Besides that; you couldn't be closer to the source of those healthy minerals and enriching temperatures.

128 HÚSAFELL CANYON BATHS

Húsafell
301 Borgarbyggð
West Iceland
+354 435 1551
husafell.com

Húsafell Canyon Baths are a treat, offering soothing warm waters in sublime surroundings and an unforgettable communal ambience. Designed by the community, a great emphasis has been put on ensuring the baths are integrated with nature. There are two pools on-site; one that boasts a temperature of 30-41°C (86-105°F), while the other is colder and more refreshing. The bathhouse has been constructed of salvaged timber from the nearby area, and the clothes hooks inside are repurposed horseshoes. Can one get anymore authentically Icelandic than this?

129 POLLURINN HOT POOL

Road 617 near
Tálknafjörður
460 Tálknafjörður
Westfjords

Known collectively as 'The Puddle', these three hot pools are found close by to the town of Tálknafjörður. Though artificial, the pools do sprout a particular green alga that can make them look unappealing at first glance. Still, there truly is no better place in the Westfjords to soak surrounded by the region's exquisite nature. A shower and changing facilities are found on-site.

130 SECRET LAGOON

Hvammsvegur
845 Flúðir
South Iceland
+354 853 3033
(tourist info)
secretlagoon.is

Constructed in 1891, the Secret Lagoon is Iceland's oldest man-made geothermal pool, hence its name Gamla Laugin (Old Pool). Built atop Hverahólmi, the active geothermal area within Flúðir town, the facilities have just recently been modernised. A lavish bar, dressing rooms, showers. Not only does the Secret Lagoon provide a rejuvenating bathing experience, but also a live geothermal area, complete with many bubbling mud pools and frothing minigeysers. During the winter, the baths close at 8 pm sharp, still leaving time for Northern Lights hunters to catch the aurora while bathing in relaxing 38-40°C water.

Embark on magical
TOURS *and* **TRIPS**

131 **ICELANDIC ELF SCHOOL**

Síðumúli 31,
2nd Fl.
108 Reykjavík
Capital Region
+354 588 6060 /
+354 894 4014
theelfschool.com

Founded in 1991, the Elf School is for those looking to learn about the mystical beings who call Iceland home. Elves, trolls, dwarves, gnomes, fairies, mountain spirits; classes leave no stone unturned, emphasising stories that tell of local Icelanders meeting such creatures. The *huldufólk* (Hidden People) are said to inhabit a parallel universe, shared by other monsters like the *afturgöngur* (Walking Again/ Zombies). Given the dangers of wandering in the wilderness, it is assumed stories of these creatures served as a warning to keep children safe in their villages.

132 **THE GHOST CENTRE**

Hafnargata 9
825 Stokkseyri
South Iceland
+354 895 0020
draugasetrid.is

There's no escaping ghoulish entities in Icelandic folklore. Take the lumbering trolls that freeze in the sunlight or the mischievous *huldufólk* who conceal their cities among the forgotten crags of the wilderness. Ghosts boast their own wicked role, as best foretold at The Ghost Centre in Stokkseyri village. As guests tread lightly through an eerie Ghost Maze, they will listen to 24 famous Icelandic ghost stories (MP3 players provided on entry), always on high alert for looming banshees in the darkness.

133 THE GIANTESS IN THE MOUNTAIN

Near Keflavik harbour
240 Reykjanesbær
South Iceland
skessan.is

Opened as part of the Night of Lights festival in 2008, this small attraction in Keflavik is for kids and adults looking to bring Icelandic folklore to life. Set in a darkened cavern nearby to the harbour, visitors follow a trail of clues until they stumble across the abode of a nameless giantess, who can be found sleeping in her rocking chair. Huge objects litter the room, from an oversized toothbrush to a grand wooden bed. The character is directly taken from the children's book, *Sigga and the Giantess*, by the beloved Icelandic writer, Herdís Egilsdóttir.

134 THE MUSEUM OF ICELANDIC SORCERY AND WITCHCRAFT

Höfðagata 8-10
510 Hólmavík
Westfjords
+354 897 6525
galdrasyning.is

The Westfjords are known for spellcraft, so it makes sense that The Museum of Icelandic Sorcery and Witchcraft would be in Hólmavík, a lovely and timeless village. Visitors will learn about ancient staves, paranormal rituals and celestial creatures through a series of gripping exhibitions. For instance, the Icelanders accused of witchcraft were typically male, an uncommon accusation elsewhere. Among the animal skulls, one can find the museum's grisly star attraction: *necropants*! To earn wealth, witches would routinely remove a man's skin from the waist down, then adorn them while keeping a gold coin in the emptied scrotum.

135 REYKJAVÍK FOLKLORE WALKING TOUR

TOUR STARTS AT:
KAMBSVEGUR

104 Reykjavík Capital Region

+354 655 4040

yourfriendin reykjavik.com

If you're looking to put what you learned at the Icelandic Elf School into practice, there is no better experience than the Reykjavik Folklore Walking Tour. After all, it is not just hidden elves that hold a special place in the Icelandic psyche, but also undead spirits said to still linger in our world. Participants will visit a real-life Elf Stone, Reykjavík's oldest cemetery, Parliament Park and the city pond, all under the direction of a historian delighted to show up the sceptics.

135 REYKJAVÍK FOLKLORE WALKING TOUR (CITY POND)

Undertake epic **JOURNEYS**

136 DRIVING HVALFJÖRÐUR / THE WHALE FJORD
Road 47, from
276 Mosfellsbær
to 301 Akranes
West Iceland
west.is

A mere half-an-hour drive from Reykavík are the majestic hillsides, inlets and panoramic views of West Iceland's Hvalfjörður (Whale Fjord). Hidden within this astounding landscape is the derelict remains of Hvítanes, a Second World War naval base, and the cascading Fossárrétt waterfall, which sits on the River Fossá and drops six metres over two cragged steps.

137 ARCTIC COAST WAY
Between 530
Hvammstangi and
685 Bakkafjörður
North Iceland
+354 462 3300
arcticcoastway.is

Having only officially opened June 2019, the Arctic Coast Way covers 900 kilometres travelling through 21 towns and 18 municipalities across the North. In other words, it's the ultimate Iceland road trip. With boat transfers included to six different islands, this route crosses into the Arctic Circle with a visit to Grímsey Island. From start to finish, there are over eight geothermal pools, as well as countless bays and peninsulas from which to seal and whale watch, or even catch the midnight sun blazing overhead.

138 THE EASTFJORDS

Road 1
East Iceland
+354 471 2320
east.is

East Iceland is a bewitching region characterised by spired mountains, winding back roads and ominous black shorelines. As the least visited and least populous region – home to only 3% of the country – the magnificent Eastfjords are a hidden blessing, providing plenty of beauty and adventure. Aside from its dramatic and primal scenery, the East also happens to be the only region where visitors can see herds of wild reindeer, a non-native species that was introduced by early Norwegian settlers for meat and leather.

139 SAILING IN BREIÐAFJÖRÐUR

Sæferðir Seatours
Smiðjustígur 3
340 Stykkishólmur
West Iceland
+354 433 2254
seatours.is

Breiðafjörður, a windswept panorama of islands that lies between the Snaefellsnes Peninsula and the Westfjords. It is simple enough to catch a ferry between these two regions, but there is no better way of experiencing this scenic stretch than through the Viking Sushi Adventure Voyage. Throughout your tour, a towed net will harvest the freshest seafood possible, offering you incredible flavours as you enjoy the pristine local surroundings. You'll be in a prime position to witness the seabirds that call the area home and, if lucky, even whales and dolphins breaching the water's surface.

140 DRIVING THE KJÖLUR HIGHLAND ROAD

**Kjalvegur,
Route F35
From Hvítá
River, 806 Selfoss
South Iceland
to Seyðisá River,
541 Blönduós
Northwest Iceland**

The mountains, canyons and glaciers of the Icelandic Highlands remain among Europe's wildest regions. A 4WD is the only means of traversing the Kjölur road – otherwise known as Kjalvegur – which penetrates this region directly, having once been used as a horse trail for those travelling between Iceland's north and south. The epic route takes about five hours to drive, passing directly between the dramatic ice caps, Langjökull and Hofsjökull.

141 HORNSTRANDIR NATURE RESERVE

TOURS DEPART FROM:
**Ísafjörður town
400 Ísafjörður
Westfjords
+354 450 8060**
westfjords.is/en

The lofty cliff sides of Látrabjarg are the Hornstrandir Nature Reserve's most iconic image, attracting not just intrepid hikers and sightseers, but also millions of nesting seabirds. Puffins, guillemots and Arctic terns all use these high elevations for protection against predators like the wily Arctic fox. Látrabjarg also marks Europe's westernmost point, making it as much a novel stop as it is beautiful. Lush, open and windswept, this reserve is an untouched paradise for those willing to make it to the Westfjords.

WILD ANIMAL *encounters*

142 SEA LIFE TRUST BELUGA WHALE SANCTUARY

Ægisgata 2
900 Westman
Islands
South Iceland
+354 488 0100
*belugasanctuary.
sealifetrust.org*

Little Grey and Little White were rescued from performance captivity for a new life in Iceland, arriving in summer 2019. A secluded bay sanctuary far more suited to their natural habitat, the belugas' sea pen is 10 metres deep and covers 32.000 square metres. During the summer, the Sea Life Trust Beluga Whale Sanctuary will be offering discrete boat trips from Klettsvík Bay that let you see Iceland's newest residents up close. On-site, visitors can also enjoy the charming aquarium and puffin rescue centre, both of which shed further light on Iceland's native species.

143 ARCTIC FOX CENTRE

Eyrardalur 1
420 Súðavík
Westfjords
+354 456 4922
melrakki.is

The Arctic fox is Iceland's only native mammal, arriving from mainland Europe over a land bridge formed during the last Ice Age. Súðavík's Arctic Fox Centre provides not only interesting display boards, artefacts and exhibitions dedicated to this fascinating species but also two actual Arctic foxes, rescued by the centre as pups. A great emphasis is placed on educating the public to threats humans pose to Arctic fox populations, including cruel practices like den-hunting and fur-farming. The best place to see Arctic foxes in the wild is either Hornstrandir Nature Reserve in the Westfjords, or the Icelandic Highlands.

144 ICELANDIC SEAL CENTER

Strandgata 1
530 Hvammstangi
Northwest Iceland
+354 451 2345
selasetur.is

Opened in 2006, the quaint exhibitions at Hvammstangi's Seal Centre delve into the eclectic wildlife that calls the Vatnsnes Peninsula home. Only harbour seals and grey seals are permanent residents, but many other species are known to drop by: bearded seals, hooded seals, ringed seals and even the odd walrus. Sustainability and environmental protection are at the forefront of the Icelandic Seal Center's work. Hopefully, we can ensure the longevity of seal colonies in Iceland for a long time to come.

145 SHEEP ROUND-UP

AT: HAMARSRÉTT
SHEEP ROUND-UP

531 Vatnsnes
Northwest Iceland
Tours: Traveo
+354 497 0800
traveo.is

Driving in Iceland, you might notice an abundance of free-roaming sheep. Set loose in the springtime, the sheep are only rounded up again when winter rolls around, continuing a practice that has lasted for centuries. There's nothing like getting your hands dirty; visitors can help out on unique tours that take you to a *réttir*, a specially designed maze fence where farmers can sort one sheep from another. If you stay an extra night at the farmstead, you can even try your hand rounding up Icelandic horses the next day.

143 **ARCTIC FOX CENTRE**

Soak up the SUMMER

146 NAUTHÓLSVÍK GEOTHERMAL BEACH

Siglunes
102 Reykjavík
Capital Region
+354 411 5330
nautholsvik.is

Iceland is not known for warm tropical beaches. The closest you'll find is Nauthólsvík, found near the Perlan Museum at the base of Öskjuhlíð Hill. With golden sandy beaches and views over Kópavogur town, swimmers can still expect fairly biting temperatures at this geothermal beach, though kids and grown-ups with a little can-do attitude will find plunging in no trouble. Lifeguards are only present at the beach during the summer. In winter, Nauthólsvík serves as an exemplary location to engage in Wim Hof-style coldwater bathing.

146 NAUTHÓLSVÍK GEOTHERMAL BEACH IN WINTER

147 NESGJÁ (SILFRA OF THE NORTH)

Between Húsavík town and Ásbyrgi Canyon
641 Húsavík
Northeast Iceland
+354 497 0800
traveo.is

Drysuit snorkelling in the glacial ravine Silfra fissure is one of Iceland's most famous and widely pursued adventure activities, but there are many other sites equally worthy of underwater exploration. Nestled away in the north of Iceland, Nesgjá spring is one such credible option. It provides crystal-clear visibility and resembles a long aquamarine corridor. Gliding along with the current, you will look at moving waves of silt and sand enclosed by monolithic rock faces, and will quickly come to appreciate this alien beauty for the rarely visited treat it is. It's only possible to go there on a guided tour as it's too dangerous to go without a guide.

148 GOLF AT CLUB BRAUTARHOLT

Kjalarnes
162 Reykjavík
Capital Region
+354 566 6045
gbr.is

Golf in Iceland? But what about the winter darkness? The snow? The erratic wind and sleet? All great questions, but playing here during summer paints a different picture entirely. A short drive from Reykjavík, Brautarholt capitalises on clear sunny days, providing rental equipment and a driving range for those looking to get on par. If you're dedicated to keeping your game sharp, be sure that a round at Brautarholt will provide you with one of the more scenic and unique games of your life. The club is open until 10 pm in the summer, allowing play under the midnight sun.

149 SPRANGAN CLIFF CLIMBING

Vestmannaeyjar
Archipelago
900 Westman
Islands
South Iceland
*visitwestman
islands.com*

Sprangan cliff climbing is not your run-of-the-mill tourist activity in Iceland, and organising a trip to the Westman Islands for this sole purpose will take some prior planning. Sprangan is a tradition in Heimaey, one that sees local islanders use simple ropes to rappel down coastal cliff sides in search of bird eggs. Swinging and swaying in the wind like pendulums, the sport has become something of a performance spectacle in itself. Classes in the summer teach families these ways of old and are now mostly practised in Skiphellar, closeby to Heimaey harbour.

150 RAFTING ON A GLACIER RIVER

Bakkaflöt
560 Varmahlíð
Northwest Iceland
+354 453 8245
bakkaflot.is

Classified as a 4+ on the international scale for river difficulty, Iceland's Austari-Jökulsá River is considered one of the most dramatic rafting sites in the world. Nicknamed 'The Beast of the East', these raging white waters provide pure exhilaration for anyone looking to conquer them. For those looking for a more relaxed rafting experience, the Jökulsárgljúfur River allows guests to float gently through a red volcanic canyon in search of bubbling hot springs.

Engage in wonderful
WINTER ACTIVITIES

151 NORTHERN LIGHTS SAILING

BOOK AT:
SPECIAL TOURS
Old Harbour
101 Reykjavík
Capital Region
+354 560 8800
specialtours.is

Many come to Iceland with the specific ambition of observing the Northern Lights. Notoriously elusive and visible only on clear dark nights, one way to maximise your chances of spotting the auroras is to take a trip with a professional agency, such as Special Tours. Known for their popular whale watching trips, this operation also departs each winter night for the blackest patches of the ocean, the perfect place to showcase Iceland's Elysian and ineffable natural light display.

152 SKI / SNOWBOARD AT BLÁFJÖLL

MEET AT: BLÁFJÖLL
PARKING LOT
111 Bláfjallavegur
203 Kópavogur
Capital Region
+354 530 3000
skidasvaedi.is

While certainly mountainous, Iceland has never been highly ranked on the pantheon of top skiing destinations, with Norway, New Zealand, France and Switzerland long having held top spots. That's not to suggest for one moment that Iceland lacks breathtaking slopes, suitable for both experienced mountaineers and complete beginners. The most convenient ski resort for most visitors is Bláfjöll; only a 25-minute drive from Reykjavík. Complete with 14 lifts, Bláfjöll operates a ski school for total novices, and is usually open from January onwards, depending on the snow. There are also several cross-country ski trails for experienced athletes.

153 SKI / SNOWBOARD AT HLÍÐARFJALL

Hlíðarfjall
600 Akureyri
Northeast Iceland
+354 462 2280
hlidarfjall.is

Another excellent spot for skiing and snowboarding is Hlíðarfjall resort, found in the north of the country. Akureyri is better known than Reykjavík for its love of snow sports – a love rivalled perhaps only by another mountainous northern town, Dalvík – and hosts the EK Extreme Ski and Snowboarding Festival each year. Residents have been skiing down Hlíðarfjall for 40 years, though current visitors have the benefit of flood-lit evening runs, snowmaking machines and 26 marked pistes.

154 ICE CAVING IN VATNAJÖKULL GLACIER

TOUR DEPARTURES AT:
Jökulsárlón
Glacier Lagoon
Parking
781 Höfn í
Hornafirði
East Iceland
+354 575 8400
vatnajokulsthjod-
gardur.is

With new sculptures and tunnels formed with each passing season, Vatnajökull's sapphire blue ice caves have long been one of the country's most alluring attractions. Caving beneath Iceland's largest glacier is about as close as one can come to stepping into a fantastical new universe; a fairytale realm that defies the imagination with its untimely grandeur and glassy interior. This tour is only available during the winter and makes for a popular side activity for many visitors travelling along Iceland's south coast.

155 DOG SLEDDING NEAR MÝVATN LAKE

Valhollt farm
641 Húsavík
Northeast Iceland
+354 847 7199
snowdogs.is

Led by howling Siberian huskies, you'll feel like an intrepid Arctic explorer speeding across the wonderful white landscapes of North Iceland. Led by a seasoned local dog-handler, sledding at Mývatn is a great opportunity to meet this special breed, as well as try your hand at a once in a lifetime activity. During the summer, this tour can be undertaken using specialised off-road carts, adding a fun twist to an already exhilarating ride.

156 SURFING ON THE SOUTH COAST

AT: ARCTIC SURFERS
Eyjarslóð 3
101 Reykjavík
Capital Region
+354 551 2555
arcticsurfers.com

Forget the cold! Who would have thought Iceland's picturesque south coast might offer prime wave breaks and surf spots? If you're a surfer, the opportunity to partake in some coldwater action is a heavy draw. Thermal protection is a must, but once out amid those waves, there can be no denying the exhilarating sense of freedom these waters provide. Surfing in Iceland should be considered essential for extreme sports lovers, with both beginner and expert-level tours provided by companies like Arctic Surfers. Surfing is available all year round, though the winter is best thanks to an influx of storms and high waves.

MOUNT VESTRAHORN

LANDSCAPES ⛰

Magnificent MOUNTAINS

157 MOUNT EINHYRNINGUR (UNICORN MOUNTAIN)
Fljótshlíð
861 Hvolsvöllur
South Iceland

As one of Iceland's more dramatic mountains, Einhyrningur's lack of visitors stems from its isolation in the Icelandic highlands. Located between the glaciers Tindfjallajökull and Mýrdalsjökull, Unicorn Mountain takes its name from a sharp, horn-like ridge rising from its northernmost slope. At 750 m, Mount Einhyrningur can be climbed with professional guidance.

158 MOUNT VESTRAHORN
Stokksnes
781 Höfn í
Hornafirði
East Iceland

Mount Vestrahorn's dragon-teeth slopes sit surrounded by the black dunes of Stokksnes Peninsula, found 16 kilometres west of the small village, Höfn. Vestrahorn appeals to all; photographers and hikers, Hollywood location scouts, or sightseers looking to experience the island's most spectacular landmarks. Given its grandeur and dominance over the landscape, this 454-metre mountain is considered one of East Iceland's most iconic peaks.

159 MOUNT HERÐUBREIÐ

ÓDÁÐAHRAUN
LAVA FIELD
661 Mývatn
Northeast Iceland

Herðubreið – Queen of the Icelandic mountains! Located on the eastern plains of Ódáðahraun desert, Herðubreið is considered one of the country's most unusual landmarks. Like Australia's Uluru, this rocky tuya bulges from the surrounding tundras as though misplaced, making it an excellent stop for landscape photographers. The slopes are so steep that the first ascent only went ahead in 1908. Nearby, the camping area Herðubreiðarlindir makes for a worthy visit, especially considering it was once used as a refuge for criminal outlaws, including the infamous bandit, Fjalla-Eyvindur, who's life was dramatised in 1911 by the Icelandic playwright, Jóhann Sigurjónsson.

160 MOUNT KEILIR

Parking by
Oddafell peak on
Höskuldarvöllur
Road
241 Grindavík
Reykjanes
Peninsula

Mount Keilir is visible when travelling across the Reykjanes Peninsula from Keflavík Airport to the capital, Reykjavík. Its distinctive cone geometry has made it a favourite spot among locals and visitors alike, making for an attractive 2-to-3-mile (3-to-5-kilometre) hike. The mountain was showcased in Baltasar Kormákur's cult comedy film, *101 Reykjavík* (2000), as the location where the titular protagonist, Hlynur, tries to unsuccessfully end his own life – (Icelandic humour can often be a little dark…).

161 MOUNT BÚLANDSTINDUR

Djúpavogshreppur
County

765 Djúpivogur
East Iceland

Towering spectacularly over two picturesque bays, the basalt pyramid Mount Búlandstindur stands at a whopping 1069 metres above sea level. For transcendental thinkers, the eight-million-year-old Búlandstindur is considered one of Iceland's major energy centres, having long been of significance to the local people. Upon the nationwide adoption of Christianity in 1000 AD, written records show how local chieftains flung their pagan idols from its slopes and cliff sides by way of proving their conversion.

Captivating CAVERNS

162 SURTSHELLIR CAVE

Surtshellir
320 Reykholt
West Iceland

Surtshellir lava cave extends nearly a mile (1,6 kilometre) beneath West Iceland's rocky black surface. For centuries, locals to the region have claimed the cave is haunted. Archaeological evidence suggests Surtshellir was often a respite for outlaws. Their presence, no doubt, fed into the already rampant paranoia felt towards this place during medieval times. Today, you're more likely to find cavers or the odd lost tourist than any bandit, and it is perfectly safe to enter with professional guides. The cave is named after the fire giant Surtr from Norse mythology.

163 RÚTSHELLIR CAVE

A short hike from
Drangshlíð 2
861 Hvolsvöllur
South Iceland
+354 483 4601
south.is

Rútshellir Cave is about as close to a hobbit house in Iceland as you can get. A small wooden abode built into the base of a massive grey cliffside, this cave is named after the troll Rútur, who was said to live here in days gone past. The site's most prominent feature, a stone barn, was built in the early 20th century. Interestingly enough, members of the German Nazi party surveyed Rútshellir Cave in 1936 believing it could be the site of a long-forgotten pagan temple.

164 KATLA ICE CAVES

TOUR MEETING POINT:
OB GAS STATION
Austurvegur 16
870 Vík í Mýrdal
South Iceland
+354 849 4404
katlatrack.is

These beautiful ice caves are located beneath Katla volcano in South Iceland. Approaching this vast and glittering network of frosty tunnels, you'll notice that much of the glacier ice is a dark grey colour because of trapped ash from past volcanic eruptions. These 3-to-4-hour ice-caving tours can only be undertaken with a guide; they will equip you with all the necessary safety gear, including a helmet-lamp and crampons.

165 LOFTHELLIR LAVA CAVE

Tour departures
from Lake Mývatn
660 Mývatn
Northeast Iceland
+354 558 8888
sagatravel.is

Three hundred seventy metres long and 3500 years old, Lofthellir Cave is near Lake Mývatn and boasts some of the grandest natural ice sculptures in the country. Stepping up close to these glassy stalagmites, you will be astounded to learn these formations occur thanks to water dripping through the ceiling for thousands of years; in other words, natural history in progress. To reach this dark Hadean realm, you will first need to walk across a rocky lava field at the base of Hverfjall volcano, so a moderate level of fitness is required to explore this site fully.

166 HELLISBÚARNIR (THE CAVE PEOPLE)

Laugarvatnshellar,
between Þingvellir
and Laugarvatn
841 Laugarvatn
South Iceland
+354 888 1922
thecavepeople.is

Hellisbúarnir was home to the last of Iceland's cave-dwelling farmers who have since moved on to greener pastures around a century ago. The home has now been rebuilt to resemble exactly how these people once lived, sheltered beneath the rock face out in Iceland's wilderness. No one is sure exactly who first built the caves; however, there are theories it was the Irish monks, known as Papar, who arrived in Iceland before the Viking Norsemen but moved on swiftly upon their arrival.

Lovely
LAKES *and* LAGOONS

167 FJALLSÁRLÓN LAGOON
Fjallsárlón
785 Öræfi
South Iceland
fjallsarlon.is

Neighbouring the famed Jökulsárlón, Fjallsárlón is a fabulous glacier lagoon in its own right, boasting terrific views of Vatnajökull ice cap. Nestled in between a steep gravel embankment and the blue wall of the glacier itself, a sailing tour on Fjallsárlón is sure to make the experience that much richer. Doing so allows you to get within touching distance of its glistening sapphire icebergs.

168 LAKE KLEIFARVATN
Parking by Road 42
241 Grindavík
Reykjanes
Peninsula

Approximately 10 square kilometres in size, Kleifarvatn is the Reykjanes Peninsula's largest lake. With no water flow in-or-out, the depth of this geothermal waterbody depends solely on groundwater. The truly adventurous can opt for a snorkelling trip in Kleifarvatn during the warmer summer months, presenting a whole new means of exploring Iceland's fascinating geography.

169 LJÓTIPOLLUR EXPLOSION CRATER
Northeast of
Frostastaðavatn
Lake
851 Hella
South Iceland

With a name directly translating to 'Ugly Puddle', one could be forgiven for believing this attraction is worth skipping over. But how wrong they would be! Located in the gorgeous Fjallabak Nature Reserve in the southern portion of the Icelandic highlands, this glittering water body is most easily visited by those trekking through the hills of Landmannalaugar.

170 LAKE LAGARFLJÓT (ALSO CALLED LÖGURINN)

Egilsstaðir
701 Egilsstaðir
East Iceland

Iceland's largest wooded area, Hallormsstaðaskógur National Forest, sits on the bank of Lake Lagarfljót, creating a lovely coniferous ambience. According to local mythos, the lake – which measures 53 square kilometres – is the watery green tomb of The Lagarfljót Wyrm, this island's Loch Ness equivalent. The snake-like creature is said to be a gigantic bottom-dweller, and many monsters-nuts swear by the b-roll capturing its movement. Either way, its speculated presence only adds to the legend and mystique of Iceland's East.

168 LAKE KLEIFARVATN

171 HÁIFOSS AND GRANNI WATERFALLS

Wet and wild **WATERFALLS**

---

171 HÁIFOSS AND GRANNI WATERFALLS

Þjórsárdalur Valley
801 Selfoss
South Iceland

Tumbling from the Stygian glacial river Þjórsá, Háifoss (High Falls) is 122 metres high, making it the fourth highest waterfall in Iceland. Granni (Neighbour) can also be seen falling majestically beside it, creating a genuinely fantastical landscape sure to leave you awestruck. Visiting these falls requires a 5 to 6-hour hike up Þjórsá's spring water tributary, Fossá, a superb experience given the agrarian surroundings of South Iceland. The most prominent landmark en route is Hekla volcano.

172 GLJÚFRABÚI (CANYON DWELLER) WATERFALL

Access from
Hamragarðar farm
861 Hvolsvöllur
South Iceland

Hidden down a narrow crack within the ancient sea cliffs of Iceland's south coast, Gljúfrabúi is a five-minute stroll from the famous waterfall, Seljalandsfoss. While the latter is best known for its trail leading visitors behind the falls, Gljúfrabúi is instantly recognisable for the mossy and monolithic rock faces that encircle the entire cascade. Getting to it will require some casual hiking as you'll need to follow a trickling stream right up to where the water drops. A natural rock platform in front of Gljúfrabúi makes for a brilliant photography spot.

173 HENGIFOSS

Parking by Road 1
701 Egilsstaðir
East Iceland
+354 471 2320
hengifoss.is

Falling 128 metres down Fljótdalsheiði cliff sides, Hengifoss (Hanging falls) was formed 5-to-6 million years ago. This feature is surrounded by red clay layers sandwiched between black lava strata, creating an out-of-this-world panorama that feels truly timeless. The waterfall is best visited alongside other eastern sites like Egilsstaðir town and Lake Lagarfljót.

174 GLUGGAFOSS WATERFALL

Fljótshlíð Area
861 Hvolsvöllur
South Iceland

Gluggafoss (Window Waterfall) is often overlooked by hurried sightseers – especially those with eyes only for South Iceland's superstars, Seljalandsfoss and Skógafoss. This is a shame considering the site's fascinating geology. Over the centuries, water has drilled holes in the malleable bedrock, creating *gluggars* (windows), through which the waterfall now flows in a series of picturesque stages.

175 DYNJANDI WATERFALL

Road 60
471 Þingeyri
Westfjords

Evocative of a large white wedding cake, Dynjandi (Thunderous) Waterfall is a multi-stage waterfall located in the very heart of the Westfjords. This breathtaking feature comprises seven separate falls which measure 100 metres high in total. Dynjandi and the surrounding area was declared a national monument in 1980 and has since become one of the region's most recognisable natural attractions.

Vehement **VOLCANOES**

176 BERSERKJAHRAUN LAVA FIELD

Helgafellssveit County

341 Snæfellsnes Peninsula

West Iceland

For Berserkjahraun's existence, we have to thank Rauðkúla, Grákúla and Kothraunskúla; three volcanoes thought to have last erupted approximately 3000 to 4000 years ago. Located between Grundarfjörður and Stykkishólmur towns, the dried remains of this epic and ancient lava flow is often considered one of Iceland's most underrated attractions. It superbly encapsulates the raw geological forces that steadily built this island. Travellers on the Snæfellsnes Peninsula should strive to see this vast area during the summer months to best appreciate the strange rock formations and colour contrasts of grey, green and brown.

177 ASKJA CALDERA
DYNGJUFJÖLL
MOUNTAINS IN
ÓDÁÐAHRAUN
LAVA FIELD
661 Mývatn
Northeast Iceland/
Central Iceland

Askja refers to open calderas found within the Dyngjufjöll mountain range. The aquamarine Víti explosion crater is the illustrative example of this attraction, drawing not only avid sightseers but also swimmers looking for truly unmatched surroundings. Lake Askja, which flows into Víti, is 220 metres deep, making it Iceland's second-largest lake behind Jökulsárlón Glacier Lagoon. Next to Lake Askja is a rock-pile monument dedicated to the German scientists Walter von Knebel and Max Rudloff who disappeared boating on the lake during a research expedition in 1907. Despite follow-up searches for the missing scientists, their bodies have yet to be recovered.

178 BRIDGE BETWEEN CONTINENTS / MIÐLÍNA
Sandvík, Road 425
233 Reykjanesbær
Reykjanes
Peninsula

Otherwise known as Miðlína, this 15-metre footbridge can be found in Reykjanes, crossing a large open ridge between the Eurasian and North American tectonic plates. A 'Welcome to Europe' and a 'Welcome to America' sign can be found hanging on both ends of the bridge, while a plaque midway reads 'In the footsteps of the Gods...'. The bridge celebrates explorer Leif Erikson, the first European thought to set foot in North America. Those who make the crossing should pick-up a personalised certificate from the Reykjavík Information Office, thus proving they made the trek from Europe to America... in theory.

179 HENGILL GEOTHERMAL AREA

Dyradalur
810 Hveragerði
South Iceland

Located between Lake Þingvallavatn and the winding main road, Suðurlandsvegur, this area at the base of Hengill Mountain boasts all that is wonderful about Icelandic nature, not the least of which are the steaming hot springs and scenic viewpoints. Both Hellisheiði Geothermal Power Plant and the Nesjavellir Power Plant sit on the periphery of this stunning site, providing a personal, if not distant look at the sustainable means by which Iceland generates the majority of its household energy.

180 LAKAGÍGAR / LAKI CRATERS

AT: VATNAJÖKULL
NATIONAL PARK
By Road 206
881 Kirkjubæjar-
klaustur
South Iceland
+354 483 4601
south.is

Formed during the 1783 Fires of the River Skaftá, one of the most violent volcanic eruptions in world history, this 27-kilometre-long series of craters known as Lakagígar make for an enticing stop while in the Southern Highlands. Pockmarked into the earth, there are 103 craters in total, best seen on a 500-metre-long visitors trail that winds through the area. Information boards en route detail more of the geological forces that caused this truly natural wonder.

Glittering **G L A C I E R S**

---

181 **DRANGAJÖKULL**
HORNSTRANDIR
NATURE RESERVE
BY ROAD 635
401 Ísafjörður
Westfjords
+354 450 8060
westfjords.is

Iceland's fifth largest glacier, Drangajökull covers 160 square kilometres in total. It is the country's northernmost glacier, located in the magical Westfjords region. Despite its size and relatively low elevation at 925 metres above sea-level, Drangajökull is the only ice cap not to have diminished in mass over the last few decades. The glacial pool that lies below it is known as Kaldalón (Cold Lagoon), often nicknamed the 'Jökulsárlón of the Westfjords'.

182 **OKJÖKULL**
Hike from
Húsafell farm
320 Reykholt
West Iceland

No longer declared a glacier, Okjökull is just one alarming example as to the threat posed by climate change. NASA has their own remembrance page for the dead ice cap, and it has also been the subject of the award-winning documentary, *Not Ok*, filmed by anthropologists Cymene Howe and Dominic Boyer. A commemorative plaque was installed on-site in 2019, written by Andri Snær Magnason and titled *A letter to the future*. In part, it reads: 'This monument is to acknowledge that we know what is happening and what needs to be done. Only you know if we did it'.

183 ÖRÆFAJÖKULL (HVANNADALSHNJÚKUR PEAK)

SKAFTAFELL NATURE
RESERVE IN
VATNAJÖKULL
NATIONAL PARK
785 Öræfi
South Iceland
+354 575 8400
*vatnajokulsthjod
gardur.is/en*

The ice-blanketed volcano Öræfajökull is notable for several reasons, the first being that it is Iceland's largest active volcano. It has not been shy in revealing its hidden powers throughout history, erupting violently both in 1362 and 1727 to 1728. The first eruption saw the destruction of the Litla-Hérað (Little Shire) district by great glacial outbursts – known as Jökulhlaups – leaving the area uninhabitable for over 40 years. This place has since become known as Öræfi (Wasteland). Located within the southern extremities of Vatnajökull National Park, Öræfajökull also boasts the country's highest peak, Hvannadalshnúkur, at 2110 metres.

183 ÖRÆFAJÖKULL (HVANNADALSHNJÚKUR PEAK)

184 SNÆFELLSJÖKULL

Stóri-Kambur
356 Snæfellsbær
West Iceland
+354 865 0061
theglacier.is

On clear days, Snæfellsjökull stratovolcano can be seen from Reykjavík, its devil horn peaks and wide sloping body a distant landmark across the blue waves of Faxaflói Bay. For those wanting a more hands-on experience, there is always the chance to ascend the mountain in true James Bond-style, meaning as a passenger in a rugged snowcat all-terrain vehicle. Your views over the rugged Snæfellsnes Peninsula will be unmatched, plus you'll be able to see up close the staggering moulins and glacial sculptures scattered across the ice cap's highest slopes. The snowcat is a pure thrill to ride inside; their huge engines are perfectly designed to work in subarctic conditions.

185 HOFSJÖKULL AND LANGJÖKULL HIKING ROUTE

Hiking route starts
at Hveravellir
Service Centre
641 Húsavík
Northeast Iceland
+354 452 4200
hveravellir.is

This 41-kilometre highlands trail lies between the glaciers Hofsjökull and Langjökull, making for a scenic 2-to-3-day hike in the Icelandic wilderness. There are four cabins en route, as well as hot pools, canyons and craters; in short, new sights and experiences around every corner. Hofsjökull (Temple glacier) is the source of Iceland's longest river, Þjórsá, while Langjökull is home to a stunning blue ice tunnel that's become a major tourist attraction in recent years. Hikers are recommended to bring their own water for the main trail.

MÓÐIR JÖRÐ

SHOPPING 🔒

Rocking RECORD SHOPS

186 KOLAPORTIÐ FLEA MARKET

Tryggvagata 19
101 Reykjavík
Capital Region
+354 562 5030
kolaportid.is

Kolaportið flea market offers many eclectic treasures, including the likes of old books and novelty sunglasses, military gear and weed pipes, fresh fish snacks and faulty electronics. It would make sense then that collectors will find quality LPs hidden within Kolaportið's stalls, providing ample hunting grounds for both vintage Icelandic music and records by mainstream artists. Open only on the weekends, Kolaportið flea market is a great stop for both music fans and lovers of kitsch goods.

187 12 TÓNAR

Skólavörðustígur 15
101 Reykjavík
Capital Region
+354 511 5656
12tonar.is

12 Tónar is a cultural gem in the heart of the city, albeit concealed behind a subtle storefront that's been left relatively unchanged since opening in 1998. Selling CDs, vinyl, clothing and specialist literature, 12 Tónar also hosts live music and poetry readings. This community store welcomes visitors with a free coffee and headphone station for playing records, making it the perfect pitstop while strolling in Reykjavík. The 12 Tónar label has released over 50 albums, with records distributed as far as Berlin, Tokyo and Seoul.

188 REYKJAVÍK RECORD SHOP

Klapparstígur 35
101 Reykjavík
Capital Region
+354 561 2299

One of the newest additions to the capital's cultural scene is the small and sophisticated Reykjavík Record Shop. Here you'll find shelves stocked with albums, including genres ranging from smooth electronic jazz to old school hip-hop. Ran by proud music aficionados, this artisan shop is also an excellent stop for picking up a record from the Icelandic music catalogue, making for a long-serving reminder of your time in this modern young city.

189 SMEKKLEYSA / BAD TAST RECORD SHOP AND LABEL

Hverfisgata 32
(Entry on Hjartatorg)
101 Reykjavík
Capital Region
+354 551 3730
smekkleysa.net

Not only is Smekkleysa (Bad Taste) one of Iceland's most famous record labels – birthing the careers of artists like Björk, the electronic-outfit, GusGus, and local rockers, HAM – but it's also a first-rate record shop. Great bands currently active today under Smekkleysa's banner include Brain Police and Sigur Rós, both titans within their genres. Smekkleysa also represents the work of late Icelandic composer, Jóhann Jóhannsson, known for his incredible scores of films such as *The Theory of Everything* (2014), *Sicario* (2015) and *Arrival* (2016).

190 GEISLADISKABÚÐ VALDA

Laugavegur 64
101 Reykjavík
Capital Region
+354 562 9002

Translating to Valdi's CD Shop, this cramped little stop looks more like a hoarder's hallway than a retail outlet. Inside is organised chaos with shelves crammed with Blu-Rays, DVDs, CDs, vinyl, cassettes, books and video games. Because of the owner's devotion to quality entertainment, this minuscule boutique is a Mecca for those anxious to add some rare finds to their collection. Shopping at this little record shop not only promises art and culture spanning the generations but also unbeatable prices that would be sacrilegious anywhere else.

191 THE ICELAND MUSEUM OF ROCK 'N' ROLL

Hjallavegur 2
260 Reykjanesbær
Reykjanes
Peninsula
+354 420 1030
rokksafn.is

"We come from the land of the ice and snow, from the midnight sun, where the hot springs flow" – The first words of Led Zeppelin's Immigrant Song, inspired by Iceland after a legendary concert here in the summer of 1970. This is just one example of Iceland's iconic place in rock history, celebrated by the modern and highly entertaining Museum of Rock n' Roll in Keflavík. It's a great place to delve deeper into this country's musical history and back-catalogue. Aside from their stock of records, guests can also buy merchandise, books and documentaries about Iceland's early rock scene.

Sumptuous SOUVENIRS

192 OMNOM CHOCOLATE FACTORY

Hólmaslóð 4
101 Reykjavík
Capital Region
+354 519 5959
omnomchocolate.com

Located at the far end of the Grandi district, Omnom Chocolate Factory has been responsible for concocting some of Iceland's most unique and delicious sweet products since 2013. Founded by childhood friends Kjartan Gíslason and Óskar Þórðarson, flavours such as 'Black n' burnt Barley' and 'Liquorice and Sea Salt' have since immortalised Omnom Chocolate as a local favourite, and a palatable surprise for visitors.

193 MÓÐIR JÖRÐ

Vallanes
701 Egilsstaðir
East Iceland
+354 471 1747
vallanes.is

Móðir Jörð (Mother Earth) focusses on growing outstanding organic products such as sweet pickled vegetables and chutneys, vegetarian burgers, breakfast barley porridge and local dried herbs. While these make for lovely souvenirs in their own right, there is perhaps no better takeaway than any one of the many jams curated at the farm, with the most popular flavours being blackcurrant, blueberry and rhubarb.

194 TULIPOP

Skólavörðustígur 43
101 Reykjavík
Capital Region
+354 519 6999
tulipop.com

Half-fantasy dreamscape, half-lifestyle brand, the nature-inspired creatures of Tulipop were first created by two friends, Signý Kolbeinsdóttir and Helga Árnadóttir. Without shying away from life's complexities, characters such as Gloomy the Mushroom Girl and the bear, Miss Maddy, populate a world that has since branched out into a Youtube animation show and book series. Picking up a Tulipop souvenir will not only spark your little one's imagination but also serve as an endearing reminder as to the magic and storytelling for which Iceland has become known.

195 BERA ICELANDIC HOT SAUCE

AVAILABLE AT
VARIOUS SHOPS
Created at
Brekka 5,
765 Djúpivogur
East Iceland
+354 820 0371
lefever.is

With its distinct fruity flavour, Iceland's first hot sauce, Bera, has proved an instant hit, providing a tingling Caribbean spice that complements a litany of meals. Cooked up by East Iceland local, William Óðinn Lefever, Bera hot sauce is made using the freshest ingredients sourced from Karlsstaðir farm in Berufjörður. Recently, they have added to their roster the new Dreki Hot Sauce, inspired by both Scandinavian and East Asian culinary traditions.

Bewitching **BOOKSHOPS**

196 BÓKAKAFFI HLÖÐUM

Helgafelli 2
700 Egilsstaðir
East Iceland
+354 471 2255
bokakaffi.is

The original bookstore Hlaðir was founded in 1973, running without disruption until 2004. In 2010, sisters Gréta and Svandís took over, transforming it into the modern and comfortable book cafe so cherished today. Bókakaffi Hlöðum is particularly favoured for its communal events, with singalongs hosted during the winter, and special weekday buffets, serving chocolate cakes and creamy waffles.

197 BÓKAVARÐAN

Klapparstígur 25-27
101 Reykjavík
Capital Region
+354 552 1710
bokiwen.is

Boasting a grand library of Icelandic and English publications, Bókavarðan is the stop for forgetful travellers who omitted packing a good holiday book. Its wide array of genres and titles suits just about anyone hoping for a literary reminder of their time in Iceland. For those inclined towards nerdier pursuits, Bókavarðan also offers a wide selection of old comic strips, films, sci-fi and fantasy novels, and is right next door to the marvellous DEAD gallery.

198 THE OLD BOOKSTORE

Hafnarstræti 3
425 Flateyri
Westfjords
+354 840 0600
flateyribookstore.com

First opened in 1920, Flateyri's only purveyor of words has remained relatively unchanged in the years since. This family business sells books by weight, allowing serious collectors to walk away with invaluable pieces of literature for just a few hundred krónas. Though mainly focussed on selling Icelandic language books, there are also books written in English, German and French.

199 BÓKAKAFFIÐ

Austurvegur 22
800 Selfoss
South Iceland
+354 482 3079
bokakaffid.
business.site

Another excellent book cafe can be found in the charming southern town of Selfoss. Complementing its shelves of printed products, Bókakaffið runs a growing publishing house known as Sæmundur, as well as an online bookstore, so visitors can feel confident in letting the booksellers make quality recommendations. Those travelling through South Iceland should make time to stop in, buy a steamy mug of coffee and lose themselves in a great book.

Creative **CLOTHING** *shops*

200 THE HANDKNITTING ASSOCIATION OF ICELAND

Skólavörðustígur 19
101 Reykjavík
Capital Region
+354 552 1890
handknitted.is

The *lopapeysa* is an iconic woollen sweater historically used by fishermen, farmers and other outdoorsmen. Nowadays, it is considered a staple part of the Icelanders' wardrobe thanks to its enduring knack for fighting off the cold. *Lopapeysas* are sold throughout the country, but there's no better place to pick one up for yourself than The Handknitting Association of Iceland. The business was formed in 1977 to maximise the unique characteristics of Icelandic sheep wool. The clothing store also sells hand-knitted gloves, hats and scarves, as well as balls of yarn and other knitting supplies.

201 KRONKRON

Laugavegur 63-B
101 Reykjavík
Capital Region
+354 562 8388
kronkron.com

As a graduate fashion designer from Paris' Studio Bercot, Hugrún Árnadóttir opened Kronkron with her partner, the hairstylist Magni Þorsteinsson, in 2004. A voguish evolution of their previous business, Kron, this new store has long aimed to expose upcoming Icelandic designers alongside their usual stock of other international collections from the likes of Vivienne Westwood and Comme des Garçons. Today, Kronkron operates on Reykjavík's principal shopping street, Laugavegur, welcoming guests with their colourful and creative designs.

202 SPÚÚTNIK

Laugavegur 28-B
101 Reykjavík
Capital Region
+354 533 2023
spuutnik
reykjavik.com

Spúútnik is at the forefront of vintage clothing in Iceland and has long bolstered the 'downtown-rat' fashion trends for which 101 Reykjavík residents have become known. The shop offers corduroy blazers and floral shirts, flat caps and moccasin shoes, as well as countless other clothing items reminiscent of bygone years. While certainly on the pricier side, Spúútnik is sure to reclaim your wardrobe and make you the flyest cat this side of the 1980s.

203 YEOMAN

Laugavegur 7
101 Reykjavík
Capital Region
+354 519 8889
hilduryeoman.com

Icelandic fashion designer, Hildur Yeoman, opened her first store in March 2017, presenting a range of womenswear that has been described as ethereal, magical and enchanting by industry peers. Hildur's collections fall back on her passion as a storyteller and illustrator, with inspiration taken from such far-flung fields as Icelandic witchcraft to the adventures of her own family. If you're looking for high-end clothing that is both elegant and celebratory, look no further than Hildur Yeoman.

204 VÍKURPRJÓN / VÍK WOOL

Austurvegur 20
870 Vík í Mýrdal
South Iceland
+354 585 8522
icewear.is

This label is one of the oldest producers of woollen attire in Iceland, a testament to its drive and authenticity, and is best known for its main product line Icewear. During a visit to the store, prospective buyers are encouraged to see the adjacent factory for themselves, revealing the entire creation process. Aside from classic woollen sweaters and accessories, Víkurprjón prides itself on the quality of its fleeces, undergarments and wide range of waterproof jackets and trousers.

RANDULFF'S SEA HOUSE

FOOD

Illustrious **I C E - C R E A M** *parlours*

205 FLÚÐASVEPPIR FARMERS BISTRO

Garðastígur 8
845 Flúðir
South Iceland
+354 519 0808
farmersbistro.is

Flúðasveppir farm's gorgeous chestnut mushrooms and bell-peppers are famous across Iceland, though there are far more novel reasons to visit for the intrepid foodie. The Farmers Bistro's strange star-attraction is mushroom ice cream, just one of the many truffle dishes on the gourmet buffet, including portobello burgers, hot soups, salads and wraps. The Secret Lagoon is just two kilometres away, making Flúðasveppir the model lunch stop after a morning spent soaking in the heat. All of Flúðasveppir's produce is grown organically in geothermal greenhouses. Make sure to pay this spot a visit during the summer.

206 EFSTIDALUR FARM

Efsti-dalur II
801 Bláskógabyggð
South Iceland
+354 486 1186
efstidalur.is

Located along the Golden Circle route, Efstidalur Farm promises plenty of unforgettable experiences. As a working horse ranch and cattle farm, riding tours can be paired with a lovely dining experience in their converted red barn, and longer tenants can appreciate an excellent night's sleep in any one of their ten comfortable dorm rooms. Best of all, Efstidalur's organic ice cream is about as fresh a dessert as one can get given it's made using milk from their own cows. If you're seeking a lunch break, Efstidalur Farm is a great choice while travelling in South Iceland.

207 CAFE LOKI

Lokastígur 28
101 Reykjavík
Capital Region
+354 466 2828
loki.is

Opposite the famous city landmark Hallgrímskirkja Lutheran church, Cafe Loki has been a local favourite for as long as Reykjavíkings care to remember. Sweet-toothed diners will have to sample the cafe's famous rye-bread ice cream, often served with pancakes or Danish-style smørrebrød sandwiches, themselves topped with herring and mashed potato. Before ice cream, visitors can sample a wealth of other Icelandic dishes, including meat soup and fermented shark – a favourite among visitors… or so the locals would have you believe!

208 VALDÍS

Grandagarður 21
101 Reykjavík
Capital Region
+354 586 8088
valdis.is

With its first parlour opened on June 1, 2013, Valdís' Italian-style ice cream has proven a fast favourite among residents and visitors alike – so much so that after only one month they had to increase their employees from 5 to 36 just to handle the demand. Many of the ice-cream flavours have been recommended directly by the customers, though all of the beloved classics are also found here, as well as a number of fruit and vegan sorbets. Valdís operates three shops (two in the capital, one in Hvolsvöllur) with plans to open more in the future.

209 BRYNJUÍS

Aðalstræti 3
600 Akureyri
Northeast Iceland
+354 462 4478

Brynjuís is to Akureyri what croissants are to Paris, what deep-dish pizza is to Chicago, what Guinness is to Dublin. Using milk instead of cream, this parlour offers delicious and iconic soft-serve ice cream. Three sizes of both waffle and cake cones with a variety of classic flavours scooped on top. The ice creams are finished with a drizzle of sauce and a crumbling of your favourite chocolate or candy. As is to be expected, Brynjuís's outdoor picnic tables make it a fabulous spot to cool off during the bright summer months.

210 SÆTA HÚSIÐ

Laugavegur 6
101 Reykjavík
Capital Region
+354 790 6939
saetahusid.is

Given the number of establishments vying for your business on Laugavegur shopping street, it's all too easy to miss this fun and fresh new ice-cream shop. Those who venture inside the cute wooden building that houses Sæta Húsið will find a plethora of unique desserts, from handmade ice-cream rolls to exquisitely baked fruit-topped cakes. In short, this is the perfect stop for a summer day's stroll around downtown Reykjavik.

Munch on hidden **H O T D O G S**

211 **SKÁL!**
AT: HLEMMUR MATHÖLL
Laugavegur 107
101 Reykjavík
Capital Region
+354 519 6515
skalrvk.com

Hot dogs are a cultural leftover from the time Iceland maintained a strong American military presence at Keflavík, but have since been reinvented by the locals. While still relatively new, Skál! has steadily built up a reputation based on its fresh takes on classic meals. Instead of competing with the famed stand, Bæjarins Beztu Pylsur, Skál's sophisticated version of the snack is worthy of praise. Topped with pickle slices and served with a Prince Polo chocolate bar, the master chefs at work in Skál! are bona fide experts when it comes to providing patrons with a more elegant bunned sausage. Skál! is located inside the food hall, Hlemmur Mathöll.

212 **ÍSBÚÐIN LAUGALÆK**
Laugalækur 8
105 Reykjavík
Capital Region
+354 561 2244

While also a fabulous ice-cream parlour in its own right, it is the hot dogs at Ísbúðin Laugalæk that draw the real crowds. This is thanks to their in-house Tröllapylsur, a twist on the German wiener that has been proudly declared the very best sausage found in the country (albeit, by them). It's also the first place to offer currywurst sausage, making this a must-stop among road-weary travellers ravenous for a Deutsch banger.

213 PYLSUVAGNINN Á AKUREYRI

Hafnarstræti
600 Akureyri
Northeast Iceland
+354 849 8827

Southern Icelanders consider their northern countrymen in Akureyri dubiously inclined when it comes to delivering delicious, albeit unhealthy and unpredictable food pairings. Prime examples of this can be found at Pylsuvagninn á Akureyri, for their speciality lies in hot dogs served with bacon, baked beans, fries, cheese or tuna. These dogs are an entire meal packaged into a single bun, delivering incredible tastes along with the quiet notion you're eating your way to cardiac arrest. Vegan sausages are also on offer, but for those who like their food big and brash, there's no takeaway more satisfying than Pylsuvagninn á Akureyri.

214 THE ICELANDIC BAR

Ingólfsstræti 1-A
101 Reykjavík
Capital Region
+354 517 6767
islenskibarinn.is

Are you fatigued by mundane meat? Sick and tired of the same old sauce? Then the Icelandic Bar's lobster hot dog is most certainly for you. Paired with the crisp local beers on tap, dinner at The Icelandic Bar is about as genuine and flavoursome cuisine as one can come across in the city. The lobster is just the beginning; other 'Not dogs' include bunned salmon with tartar sauce (paired with Viking lager), deep-fried shrimp with spicy mayonnaise (with Pils Organic) and lamb and bearnaise sauce (with Viking Stout).

211 **SKÁL!**

214 **THE ICELANDIC BAR**

215 BÆJARINS BEZTU PYLSUR

Tryggvagata 1
101 Reykjavík
Capital Region
+354 511 1566
bbp.is

Admittedly, Bæjarins Beztu is not much of a secret given its longstanding reign as Iceland's main provider of delicious hot dogs, having started in 1937. Yet, no guidebook on Iceland could be considered complete without mentioning how they've transformed this American dish into a bona fide local classic. Bæjarins Beztu serves bunned sausages made of lamb, beef and pork, topped with specially curated condiments and crunchy onions. As a testament to their popularity, you'll no doubt see long queues that stretch out into the street, as well as picnic tables for outdoor eating.

Enjoy lavish **L U N C H** *breaks*

216 **KAFFI KYRRÐ**
Skúlagata 13
310 Borgarnes
West Iceland
+354 437 1878
blomasetrid.is

As a colourful family-run establishment emphasising homeliness and tranquility for its guests, Kaffi Kyrrð is a must-visit for any traveller passing through Borgarnes. Luscious plantlife, local art and statues of the Buddha dot the premises, which feels as wild and welcoming as the eclectic menu offered. Cakes, coffees, soups, sandwiches and multiple vegan options all make Kaffi Kyrrð worth your time. If you're looking to extend your stay in Borgarnes, you are invited to check out the cosy guesthouse run in tandem with the cafe.

217 **TEHÚSIÐ HOSTEL, CAFE & BAR**
Kaupvangur 17
700 Egilsstaðir
East Iceland
+354 471 2450
tehusidhostel.is

Aside from its environmental consciousness, Tehúsið hostel prides itself on two things; its wide selection of quality Icelandic beers, and the fresh, organic ingredients used in their beloved local delicacies. Located just beside Egilsstaðir campsite, this family-run hostel also offers an events cinema, regular live music and even free-to-play instruments. The Hostel Geeks website voted Tehúsið as among Iceland's best hostels in 2020.

218 NORÐ AUSTUR

Norðurgata 2
710 Seyðisfjörður
East Iceland
+354 787 4000
nordaustur.is

Iceland is famous for its abundance of fresh fish, yet attempts to capitalise on its own style of sushi still remain largely wanting. Thankfully, the Seyðisfjörður restaurant, Norð Austur, has long swum against the current by offering locally sourced sushi so delicious it threatens to rival even their Japanese counterparts. Alongside an appetising and colourful variety of beverages (daiginjo sake, being one example), diners can sample smoked arctic char, Japanese fried chicken and spicy salmon rolls.

219 VOGAFJÓS FARM RESORT

Vogum 1
660 Mývatn
Northeast Iceland
+354 464 3800
vogafjosfarmresort.is

Homemade cheese and baked goods, hanged meat and smoked trout are just some of the mouth-watering delicacies cooked up at Vogafjós Farm Resort. Both a guesthouse and cafe-restaurant, this delightful retreat has been in the same family for 120 years. Visitors will meet the farm's sheep and cows and can purchase artisan products at the market stall inside the barn.

220 CAFÉ RIIS

Hafnarbraut 39
510 Hólmavík
Westfjords
+354 451 3567
caferiss.is

Sit back and relax in this attractive homespun pub, where magic runic symbols are carved decoratively in the bar, and elk antlers hang above the front door. Aside from the staple menu items like grilled strips of teriyaki chicken and fried cod chins, Café Riis also serves a range of artisan pizzas, making it a fine choice for both fine dining and a quick dinner stop. Anyone venturing as far as the majestic Westfjords should stop by while passing through the Hólmavík; you'll recognise Café Riis in the centre of town by its lime-green, corrugated iron exterior.

221 BAUTINN RESTAURANT

Hafnarstræti 92
600 Akureyri
Northeast Iceland
+354 462 1818
bautinn.is

With reasonable prices and countless praising reviews, it seems that Bautinn will forever be one of Akureyri's most cherished restaurants. Instantly recognisable thanks to its bright red paint job, patrons can enjoy quality dishes like sirloin steaks, lobster bisque and lamb chops, all with a cold beer or glass of wine. Despite its nickname, the 'Northern Capital', Akureyri has only a handful of fine dining restaurants, which makes visiting Bautinn an excellent choice for those looking for family-friendly dining. Open daily from 11 am; the restaurant is located in one of Akyureyri's oldest buildings, dating back to 1902.

222 KAFFI LAUGALÆKUR

Laugarnesvegur 74-A
105 Reykjavík
Capital Region
+354 537 6556
laekur.is

Kaffi Laugalækur is located in Laugardalur, a district of Reykjavík where residents once washed their clothes using the geothermal pools so abundant in the area. The bright green Kaffi Laugalækur serves a wide variety of dishes, including, but not limited to smoked trout bake, shawarma lamb, hashed fish and chorizo calzone. The cafe makes for a great stop after taking a dip at the nearby pool, Laugardalslaug, which is the biggest swimming complex in the country.

Savour these blissful **BAKERIES**

---

223 **REYNIR BAKARI**

Dalvegur 4
200 Kópavogur
Capital Region
+354 564 4700
reynirbakari.is

On top of the classic Icelandic desserts and pastries offered, Kópavogur's Reynir bakari has long strived to explore new avenues in the world of baking, most recently with its sugar-free sourdough bread, lovingly made with Icelandic rapeseed oil and a healthy dollop of artisan expertise. Open every day of the week, Reynir bakari also specialises in selling chocolates, cakes, marzipan turnovers and creamy tartlets. If you decide to stop by at either of Reynir bakari's branches in Kópavogur, make sure to do it early before they sell out of their famous German bread buns.

224 **SANDHOLT**

Laugavegur 36
101 Reykjavík
Capital Region
+354 551 3524
sandholt.is

Operated by fourth-generation artisan bakers, Sandholt is among the oldest bakeries in Iceland and is today advantageously located on Reykjavík's main shopping street, Laugavegur. Several types of sourdough bread are displayed alongside quality pastries, boxed chocolates and jam-packed sandwiches, including the likes of pulled pork, serrano ham and smoked arctic char. To make your visit more worthwhile, Sandholt also offers a delicious selection of craft-brew beers, ciders and wines, cloudy and unfiltered so as to best emote an authentically homespun taste.

225 HEIMABAKARÍ

Garðarsbraut 15
640 Húsavík
Northeast Iceland
+354 464 2901
heimabakri.is

Opening early each morning, Heimabakarí is the first place guests to Húsavík should be heading for a sandwich and coffee, heartily recommended before embarking on one of the village's famed whale watching trips. With a range of products baked fresh every morning, patrons are free to enjoy their purchases in the cafe's comfortable interior or take them away to enjoy while strolling around the beachheads of the Northeast.

226 MOSFELLSBAKARÍ

Háholti 13-15
270 Mosfellsbær
Capital Region
+354 566 6145
mosfellsbakari.is

Opened in 1982, Mosfellsbakarí has become known not just for its wide selection of pastries, cakes and sandwiches, but also its homemade lace chocolate, created by the foreign-trained master chocolatier, Hafliði Ragnarsson. Mosfellsbakarí is advantageously located for tourists on the move, drawing back return customers year after year. If you're hungry enough to be among them, make a stop before embarking north on the Ring Road or the Golden Circle route.

Eat scintillating **S E A F O O D**

227 RANDULFF'S SEA HOUSE

Strandgötu 96
735 Eskifjörður
East Iceland
+364 477 1247
+354 696 0809
randulffsjohus.is

Offering shark meat and locally caught fish, Randulff's Sea House has remained relatively unchanged since its 1890 construction on the Eskifjörður fjord's shoreline. Diners can appreciate the decorative artefacts that linger from the late 19th and 20th century; a period considered the golden age of fishing for East Iceland. Built by the Norwegian Peter Randulff, the building was used for storing herring until stocks dried in the 1950s. The house remained out of use for 75 years until being partly purchased by the East Iceland Maritime Museum, who helped renovate it into the restaurant we see today.

228 SALKA VALKA

Skólavörðustígur 23
101 Reykjavík
Capital Region
+354 571 1289
salkakitchen.com

Located on Skólavörðustígur – the rainbow street leading up to Hallgrímskirkja church – this delightful eatery promises signature Icelandic dishes, including *plokkfiskur*, fish stew and classic fish and chips. A colourful interior paired with a fresh menu and careful selection of local beers make this a sure dinner choice any time of the year, plus desserts like rhubarb cake only adds to the promise. The restaurant is named after a novel by the Icelandic Nobel laureate, Halldór Laxness.

229 HEIMAHUMAR LOCAL LANGOUSTINE TRUCK

Jökulsárlón
parking lot
781 Höfn í
Hornafirði
East Iceland
+354 891 6250

If you could add one thing to Iceland's picture-perfect nature, what would it be? Fast food, of course! Only the fresh taste of lobster could make a visit to Jökulsárlón glacier lagoon all the more worthwhile. Thankfully, Heimahumar Local Langoustine Truck has you covered with its range of crustacean-based cuisine. While looking out over this incredible, iceberg-filled glacier lake, hungry travellers can choose from such tasty options as lobster rolls or wraps, hot soups and toasted 'lobster dogs'. If ever anyone needed one more reason to visit Iceland's star attraction, this langoustine truck would be it.

230 PAKKHÚS RESTAURANT

Krosseyjarvegur 3
780 Höfn í
Hornafirði
East Iceland
+354 478 2280
pakkhus.is

Overlooking Höfn's harbour, the tantalising Pakkhús Restaurant was originally built in 1932 as a warehouse but today is a quality eatery focussed on sourcing and utilising the very best ingredients from the Vatnajökull region. Höfn is particularly famed for its Icelandic lobster, caught routinely on the red ship, Sigurður Ólafsson SF44, often seen resting in the town's idyllic harbour. This makes eating the restaurant's seafood a particularly authentic experience, given one can see the entire process from the sea to the plate.

231 NAUSTIÐ

Ásgarðsvegi 1
640 Húsavík
Northeast Iceland
+354 464 1520

Unmissable thanks to its bright yellow paint, Naustið restaurant provides home-baked treats, meats from local farms and homegrown vegetables, culminating in homely and comforting food hard to get elsewhere in the Northeast. Naustið is particularly admired for its signature fish soup, and 'mashed fish', once considered a staple of poverty-stricken Icelanders, but now reborn as one of the country's most nurturing dishes.

229 HEIMAHUMAR LOCAL LANGOUSTINE TRUCK

Taste-test
TRADITIONAL TREATS

---

232 FJÖRUKRÁIN
Vikingastræti 1-3
220 Hafnarfjörður
Capital Region
+354 565 1213
fjorukrain.is

Given its old-timey Norse architecture, Fjörukráin in Hafnarfjörður is nicknamed 'The Viking House' and is located in the town's second-oldest building, initially constructed in 1841. Open every day from 6 pm to 10 pm, waiters adorned in medieval attire serve a range of traditional meals, including lamb shanks and dried haddock. Though a little way out of Reykjavík, most visitors to Iceland will pass this instantly recognisable building when taking the airport shuttle from Keflavík.

233 BJARNARHÖFN SHARK MUSEUM
Bjarnarhöfn
341 Stykkishólmur
West Iceland
+354 438 1581
bjarnarhofn.is/

The Snæfellsnes Peninsula is still the island's largest producer of *hákarl*, that infamous Icelandic cuisine better known as fermented (or rotten) Greenland shark. Bjarnarhöfn Shark Museum is the best place to not only taste-test this highly contentious food but also learn more about the hunting and fermenting procedure. Visitors will also see historic fishing boats, as well as stunning exhibitions that display shark-fishing tools and gear.

234 REYKJAVÍK FOOD HALL

Vesturgata 2
101 Reykjavík
Capital Region

The Reykjavík Food Hall is in a stand-out yellow building downtown and can trace its history to 1863 when it was built to serve as an office and warehouse for the mail service, though quickly became a hangout for sailors and merchants. In the past, the building has also been used as an entertainment venue, cafe and publishers. Today, guests can enjoy sublime local dishes from a variety of vendors. Stand up for a quick bite, or sit down and stay awhile, just make sure you pop in to this new inner-city food hub.

235 KAFFIVAGNINN

Grandagarður 10
101 Reykjavík
Capital Region
+354 551 5932
kaffivagninn.is

Iceland's oldest restaurant, Kaffivagninn, is still going strong, remaining relatively unchanged since renovations in 1975. Its roots can be traced back to 1935 when the founder Bjarni Kristjánsson ran his menu off a small food truck, known even then as 'The Coffee Wagon'. Kaffivagninn is now permanently established on the harbour at Grandi and is open seven days a week. Locals would recommend traditional dishes like the fish platter or *plokkfiskur*, though its hot breakfast offerings also come highly praised.

Appreciate **FINE DINING**

236 **KOPAR**

Geirsgata 3
101 Reykjavík
Capital Region
+354 567 2700
koparrestaurant.is

Situated in the green houses at Old Harbour, Kopar is a restaurant owned by chef Ylfa Helgadóttir and wine-expert Ásta Guðrún Óskarsdóttir. Kopar is praised for their new-wave and traditional cocktails, though others may choose to enjoy their series of cognacs and whiskies, referred to as the Icelandic Fisherman's Collection. When it comes to food, Kopar is the first restaurant to serve Icelandic rock crab, alongside a plethora of other delicious dishes, including grilled reindeer, zucchini with chickpeas and raw Breiðafjörður scallops.

237 **NORDIC RESTAURANT**

Norðurgata 2
710 Seyðisfjörður
East Iceland
+354 472 1277
hotelalden.is

A candlelit ambience and Cordon Bleu cooking culminate at Nordic Restaurant in Seyðisfjörður. Sourcing its vegetables from Vallanes ecological farm, and its lamb from the East-Icelandic plateau, it is now among the country's most reputable eateries. First opened in 2003 under Hotel Aldan's management, this fine dining establishment takes inspiration from local trends while also serving its lip-smacking twist on Danish, French and Italian cuisine. The restaurant is housed in one of Iceland's oldest shops, with the original interior still intact.

238 FJÖRUBORÐIÐ

Eyrarbraut 3-A
825 Stokkseyri
South Iceland
+354 483 1550
fjorubordid.is

Cooked with passion, flair and zeal, Fjöruborðið offers three kinds of locally caught lobster. The sophisticated restaurant, nestled on the coastline of Stokkseyri town, is the perfect place for guests to sip on top-notch lobster bisques in a homely atmosphere decorated with marine memorabilia. Little wonder this restaurant has been critically applauded as 'the gourmet sanctuary of the South'.

239 MATHÚS GARÐABÆJAR

Garðatorg 4-B
210 Garðabær
Capital Region
+354 571 3775
mathus.is

In the heart of Garðabær, this first-class restaurant promotes a variable menu-plan consisting of fish, meat and soup, all of which is freshly prepared from organic ingredients. With French and American twists, this sleek and modern establishment remains true to its Icelandic brasserie traditions, as well as placing great emphasis on the well-being of its young guests, with a separate room for children to play unencumbered by adult conversation. Garðabær is a district of Reykjavík rarely visited by tourists, making Mathús Garðabæjar something of an overlooked gem by foreign visitors.

240 VON MATHÚS & BAR

Strandgata 75
220 Hafnarfjörður
Capital Region
+354 583 6000
vonmathus.is

Von Mathús interweaves delicious seasonal food, a homely atmosphere and professional service with pure finesse. Most guests swear by the five-course menu, with such tantalising dishes as cured sea trout, tender ox cheek and for dessert, blood orange with white chocolate ganache, paired with selected wines. A couple-run establishment; chef Einar and manager Kristjana named their restaurant Von (Hope), in part because it seems so fitting to the general mood and ambience of Hafnarfjörður's port area.

241 KOL RESTAURANT

Skólavörðustígur 40
101 Reykjavík
Capital Region
+354 517 7474
kolrestaurant.is/

A 3-minute walk from Hallgrímskirkja church, this two-floor restaurant sports an open kitchen and modern decor. Kol's Scandinavian cuisine is masterminded by one of Reykjavík's most promising young chefs, Sævar Lárusson. Patrons can expect juicy steaks, garden-fresh salads and locally sourced seafood, best enjoyed with a fruity cocktail in hand.

242 NIELSEN RESTAURANT

Tjarnarbraut 1
700 Egilsstaðir
East Iceland
+354 471 2001
nielsenrestaurant.is

With an open balcony and verdant terrace available during the summer, the much-loved Nielsen Restaurant is fantastic for either a quick coffee or a full meal. After all, quality service has been central to their philosophy since first opening in 1996. Situated in Egilsstaðir's oldest house – built by the Danish trader Oswald Nielsen in 1944 – the menu boasts such delights as lobster soup, reindeer nachos, and BBQ ribs, as well as a litany of home baked pastries and cakes.

Visit **VEGAN &**
VEGETARIAN *friendly restaurants*

---

243 **ÍSLENSKA FLATBAKAN**

Bæjarlind 2
201 Kópavogur
Capital Region
+354 567 1717
flatbakan.is

Piping hot Italian food is Íslenska Flatbakan's speciality. This pizzeria has made a name for itself in recent years, offering a wide range of toppings and lip-smacking sides in comfortable surroundings. If meat is not your style, there are six vegan pizzas on the menu, as well as a vegan dessert pizza, and you can be confident that Íslenska Flatbakan has sought to make an impact in this area since first opening its doors. Those who sign up on Facebook as friends of Íslenska Flatbakan are even offered first taste-testing rights on new vegan dishes from the kitchen.

244 **JUNKYARD FOOD TRUCK**

Skeifan 13-A
108 Reykjavík
Capital Region
+354 694 5276
bestjunkintown.is

'Junk' typically implies food is not particularly healthy, nor sophisticated upon serving. Well, think again, for this local food truck company has turned perceptions on their head, offering a fantastic vegan menu that provides such meals as burgers and chips, roast-potato wraps, salads and fruit smoothies. Given the fact Junkyard is a travelling food truck, make sure to keep up to date on their social media channels to find where they'll be setting up shop on any given day.

245 THE SOUP COMPANY

Víkurbraut 5
870 Vik í Mýrdal
South Iceland
+354 778 9717
thesoupcompany
iceland.com

Nothing beats the nurturing flavours of hot soup on a stormy day. The Soup Company at Vík provides this comfort by the bowlful, offering a variety of delicious soups each served with a side of freshly baked bread. Vegetarians can order the pesto-doused tomato and mozzarella baguette or a steamy potion of vegan soup. There are also plenty of meat options available for those who prefer.

246 KAFFIHÚSIÐ GARÐURINN

Klapparstígur 37
101 Reykjavík
Capital Region
+354 561 2345
kaffigardurinn.is

Both a restaurant-cafe and greengrocer, Kaffihúsið Garðurinn has been going strong since 2000 and is considered by locals to be, perhaps, the tastiest vegetarian stop in Reykjavík. Their Italian vegetable soups are particularly favoured, though you'll find all their dishes are generously served, and priced very reasonably for Iceland. Kaffihúsið Garðurinn has a history of daily menu changes, so is well-suited to an audacious bon vivant looking for high-calibre vegetarian food.

247 BIKE CAVE

Einarsnes 36
101 Reykjavík
Capital Region
+354 770 3113
bikecave.is

Located on a popular cycling lane along Reykjavík's coast, Bike Cave is a homestyle joint that prides itself on a nutritious and increasingly varied menu. Its juicy burgers, stuffed sandwiches and plentiful pitas are just a handful of the menu choices that can be adapted to a vegan diet. Whatever dish you choose, you'll find Bike Cave's offerings are best enjoyed with a warming cup of tea or coffee. The staff happily oblige those with specific dietary requirements and even offer tools and equipment to rent for those who wish to use the cafe as a cycling pitstop.

Chow down on **C H E A P B I T E S**

248 BASTARD BREW & FOOD

Vegamótastígur 4
101 Reykjavík
Capital Region
+354 558 0800
bastard.is

Bastard Brew & Food dishes up surprisingly ample portions on the cheap, making it a filling go-to for visitors in downtown Reykjavík. Small dishes perfect for sharing include tiger prawns, nachos with cheese dip, loaves of garlic bread, hummus and pesto, while single mains shift focus to meaty burgers, flatbreads and soft tacos. During summer, the outside porch is a relaxed spot for enjoying cocktails in good company. Bastard Brew & Food is decked out with hip and avant-garde paintings and often themes its menus according to the weekday, such as Taco Tuesdays and Gin & Tonic Wednesdays.

249 VIÐ VOGINN

Vogaland 2
765 Djúpivogur
East Iceland
+354 478 8860
vidvoginn.is

A practical and charming stop for any traveller with extra time, Við Voginn in Djúpivogur supplies excellent comfort food; hot meals, cold pastries, cakes, all paired with impressive views over the town's yacht-filled harbour. Reasonably priced, Við Voginn is one of the prime spots for buying such classics as a cheeseburger and fries, hot dogs (vegan options available) and chicken or beef pitas, not to mention the coffees, homemade cakes and freshly baked cookies.

250 NOODLE STATION

Laugavegur 103
101 Reykjavík
Capital Region
+354 551 3198
noodlestation.is

Noodle Station remains true to its Thai roots, keeping things simple with their three delicious broths; noodle soup with beef, noodle soup with chicken and noodle soup with vegetables, all cooked up with a litany of secret spices. Mouth-watering smells emanate from the restaurant front, providing those exiting Hlemmur bus station with the irresistible temptation to eat. The recipes have been in the family of Noodle Station founder, Charin Thaiprasert, for generations.

251 DJ GRILL

Strandgata 11
600 Akureyri
Northeast Iceland
+354 462 1800
djgrill.is

DJ Grill is a burger restaurant utterly dedicated to its craft! Aside from providing a meaty range of succulent burger meals – named after former disc jockeys popular in Akureyri at the time of opening – DJ Grill is also a dedicated sports bar and should be mainly visited by fans of English football. Do note; Arsenal games take precedence on the screen, showing each and every game played by the Gunners without exception.

252 SKÚRINN

Aðalgata 25
340 Stykkishólmur
West Iceland
+354 544 4004

Skúrinn proudly declares itself 'a bad place for a diet', and with one look at the menu, you'll realise nothing could be more true. Located in the heart of Stykkishólmur, a picturesque fishing town on the Snaefellsnes Peninsula, guests can expect a hearty selection of burgers, beers and wraps. While this local favourite might not look much from the outside, situated next door to a petrol station, the allure of delicious and quickly served American-style cuisine is sure to draw you inside.

253 TJÖRUHÚSIÐ

Neðstakaupstað
400 Ísafjörður
Westfjords
+354 456 4419
tjoruhusid.is

With children under 14 permitted to eat for free, a visit to the family-run Tjöruhúsið restaurant in Ísafjörður is one surefire way to go easy on the purse strings. The restaurant forgoes a menu in place of serving the day's freshest catch, be it cod, halibut, wolffish, spotted catfish or redfish. The restaurant is also known for serving flavoursome Indian food on certain nights.

254 FREDERIKSEN ALE HOUSE

Hafnarstræti 5
101 Reykjavík
Capital Region
+354 571 0055
frederiksen.is

Prudent on prices, Frederiksen Ale House is a modern gastropub just minutes from Reykjavík's Old Harbour and Ingólfstorg Square. Opened in 2014 with the goal of taking comfort food to a new gastric level, the main reason to go is the hearty meal portions and the excellent beer and wine selection (2-for-1 specials at happy hour). Those looking for a quick and inexpensive burger or fish and chips will do no better than this alehouse.

254 FREDERIKSEN ALE HOUSE

SKÚLI CRAFT BAR

DRINK 🍷

Chat in COMFY CAFES

255 KAFFI KLAUSTUR

Skriðuklaustur
701 Egilsstaðir
East Iceland
+354 471 2990
skriduklaustur.is

Housed in the cultural centre Skriðuklaustur – former quarters of the revered Icelandic author, Gunnar Gunnarsson – Kaffi Klaustur is one of East Iceland's finest casual cafes. Focussed on providing excellent coffee and flavoursome regional cuisine, Kaffi Klaustur will leave no traveller hungry with their very generous daily lunch buffets. Expect such appetising offerings as Icelandic lamb, venison, bramble berries and sauteed mushrooms.

256 GRÁI KÖTTURINN / THE GREY CAT

Hverfisgata 16-A
101 Reykjavík
Capital Region
+354 551 1544
graikotturinn.is

Those facing untimely arrivals to the city can do no better than Grái Kötturinn, a delightful stop to enjoy the early morning hours with a large cup of piping hot *svart kaffi* (black coffee). Guests seeking a hearty breakfast need look no further than the staple menu item, The Truck: American pancakes, potatoes, fried eggs, toast, bacon and tomatoes. Stopping by Grái Kötturinn is a nourishing way to begin your day exploring the city.

257 KATTAKAFFIHÚSIÐ

Bergstaðastræti 10-A
101 Reykjavík
Capital Region
kattakaffihusid.is

Cats, coffee and comfortable surroundings; Kattakaffihúsið has capitalised on the popularity of cat cafes abroad, allowing patrons the chance to stroke a furry friend as they sip on foamy lattes and creamy macchiatos. Kattakaffihúsið's close working relationship with Iceland's animal rescue service, Dýrahjálp, has provided these moggies with a second chance at life. Further compassion is evident in their vegan-friendly menu; such options as sourdough bread with grilled avocado or oat yoghurt with berry sauce can all be sampled here under the apathetic gaze of our feline overlords.

258 CAFÉ ROSENBERG

Vesturgata 3
101 Reykjavík
Capital Region
+354 546 1842
cafe-rosenberg.
business.site

Boasting a warm and homely ambience, Café Rosenberg is split between two floors; the first is a stylish, spacious tearoom where cakes, sandwiches and hot coffee stand temptingly on display. The basement, on the other hand, caters as a quiet place to chat or study over a cold lager. Rosenberg is particularly known for its popular board game nights; chess and checkers, Dungeons & Dragons, Monopoly, Poker and so much more. Make sure to join in on the casual hijinks during one of your quieter nights in the capital.

Drink at **PERFECT PUBS** *and* **CRAFT BARS**

---

259 **THE SALT CELLAR**
Near Hotel Flatey
Stóra-Pakkhús
345 Flatey Island
West Iceland
+354 555 7788
hotelflatey.is

Beer in Iceland was illegal until the long-overdue year of 1989, but today, golden and refreshing pints can be found across the island. This is true even when talking of its remotest spots, of which there is no better example than The Salt Cellar on Flatey Island. As its name suggests, this minuscule pub was used for storing salt barrels for traders and fishermen since at least the early 1900s. Visitors today can enjoy a decent pint or the Flahajito, Flatey Island's take on the classic mojito.

260 **SKÚLI – CRAFT BAR**
Aðalstræti 9
101 Reykjavík
Capital Region
+354 519 6455

Purveyors of excellent ales and artisan lagers need to look no further than Skúli - Craft Bar, a welcoming public house with over 130 brands on offer, including 14 craft beers on tap. Bartenders will happily allow patrons the chance to taste the various booze on offer. For those who want to down the very best samples, 4500 ISK will provide you with a quality six-beer platter – by far the best means to kick off a fun night in Reykjavík that you'll never remember!

261 STRIKIÐ

**Skipagata 14,
5th Fl.
600 Akureyri
Northeast Iceland
+354 462 7100**
strikid.is

With an elaborate menu offering fresh seafood (with a particular emphasis on sushi), Strikið is one of Akureyri's most elegant gastropubs. Aside from the food menu – offering the likes of sake chicken, grilled beef tenderloin and BBQ baby back ribs – guests can enjoy a variety of fruity cocktails and thirst-quenching wines. Strikið is the perfect place to sit back, relax and sip on some fine hooch, with its spacious balcony promising wonderful views over Eyjafjörður fjord, Akureyri, and the surrounding ocean and mountains.

262 GRAND-INN BAR AND BED

**Aðalgata 19
550 Sauðárkrókur
Northwest Iceland
+354 844 5616**

Grand-Inn Bar and Bed is a cosy spot to grab a locally brewed beer or one of the many international craft brews on tap. The bar regularly hosts live events, as well as plays live sports on its TV screens, and its walls are decorated with humorous artwork by the Icelandic cartoonist, Hugleikur Dagsson. This establishment, which was previously awarded 'Best Bar in North Iceland' by The Reykjavik Grapevine, also operates as a guesthouse, offering five spacious rooms.

263 GÖTUBARINN

Hafnarstræti 96
600 Akureyri
Northeast Iceland
+354 462 4747
gotubarinn.is

A downstairs piano only adds to the homely charm of Götubarinn, a bar in Akureyri centre much beloved by local revellers. Reminiscent of the old city's architecture, the bar has a rustic timber interior decorated with street signs and mirrors, making it an intimate spot for deep-seated conversations or even the occasional sing-along. Götubarinn is split over two floors, closes late and offers a wide selection of alcoholic and non-alcoholic drinks, thus flourishing as a prime example of Akureyri's nightlife. You'll recognise the bar instantly thanks to its bright blue woodwork outside.

264 BELJANDI BRUGGHÚS

Sólvellir 23
760 Breiðdalsvík
East Iceland
+354 866 8330
beljandibrugghus.is

A microbrewery in a micro town, a small yet delicious range of beers has been on offer ever since Beljandi Brugghús first opened in 2017. The operation takes its name from its signature pale ale Beljandi, though other notable beverages include the porter, Skuggi, and IPA, Spaði. Their beers are also available in certain bars in Reykjavík, namely Karólína Craft Bar and Cafe.

Bask at Reykjavík
ROOFTOP BARS

---

265 PETERSEN SVÍTAN

Ingólfsstræti 2-A
101 Reykjavík
Capital Region
+354 563 4000
gamlabio.is

Petersen Svítan was formerly a third-storey apartment; the space has now been renovated into one of the capital's tallest and most sought-out taphouses. Views over the bustling streets below make drinking here as much of a cosmopolitan affair as possible in Iceland. Gamla Bíó venue (a former cinema, and now used as an opera house and theatre) is located just downstairs, so Petersen Svítan is a convenient spot to stop for a drink after taking in a concert or theatre show.

266 SKY RESTAURANT & BAR

Ingólfsstræti 1
101 Reykjavík
Capital Region
+354 595 8545
skyreykjavík.com

On Center Hotel Arnarhvoll's 8th floor sits SKY Restaurant & Bar, a beloved establishment thanks to its elegant veranda that provides guests with marvellous views over Old Harbour, Harpa Concert Hall and Faxaflói Bay. There is an excellent selection of wines, beers and cognacs on offer, best enjoyed with the listed bar snacks: cheddar cubes, mixed nuts and serano ham.

267 LOFT HI HOSTEL

Bankastræti 7
101 Reykjavík
Capital Region
+354 553 8140
hostel.is

Loft HI Hostel's inside sports an abundance of bookshelves, thus is a good spot for avid readers, stressed-out students or just about anyone looking for a beverage in relative quiet. Loft Hostel's biggest draw, however, is its glorious rooftop from where guests have a great bird's-eye view over Laugavegur and the city skyline. Throughout the year, Loft Hostel is known for hosting several community nights, from watercolour classes, a clothes swap & shop, and even intimate music and stand-up comedy performances.

268 LEBOWSKI BAR

Laugavegur 20-A
101 Reykjavík
Capital Region
+354 552 2300
lebowskibar.is

Attention Dudes & Dudettes! Lebowski Bar is one of the coolest novelty bars in Reykjavík. The rooftop is only open during the summer, but the rug-draped walls and movie posters of its interior manage to really tie the room together. In line with the cult comedy classic, patrons can choose from a variety of White Russian cocktails, as well as take part in the pub quizzes and parties celebrated throughout the year. And, if on the off chance, Lebowski Bar doesn't meet your expectations, remember that's just, like, your opinion, man.

Bountiful **BREWERIES** and **DISTILLERIES**

269 **EIMVERK DISTILLERY**
Lyngás 13
210 Garðabær
Capital Region
+354 416 3000
flokiwhisky.is

A tour of Eimverk Distillery will not only provide you with insight into how quality spirits are made but also serves as the best means of sampling these bottled treasures yourself. Derived from organic Icelandic barley, Flóki is both Eimverk Distillery's premium product and the island's first single malt whiskey. After four years of experimentation and 163 trials, Flóki is now matured in American oak barrels to boost a complex and earthy flavour, reminiscent of Irish and Scottish Highland whiskeys. Other drinks include a premium gin, Vor, and aquavit (or *brennivín*) named Víti.

270 **ASKUR TAPROOM, BAR & BREWERY**
Fagradalsbraut 25
700 Egilsstaðir
East Iceland
+354 470 6070
askurtaproom.is

Open since March 2018, Askur Taproom is available to explore by pre-booked tours throughout the year, meaning some preparation is necessary before your visit. However, touring the premises promises a cultural experience quite unlike any other, for not only will you learn about the fascinating process of creating original beers from scratch, but you'll also try out delicious custom-made pizzas.

271 BJÓRSETUR ÍSLANDS / THE ICELANDIC BEER CENTRE

Hólar
551 Hólar
Northwest Iceland

Operated on a purely voluntary basis by staff members from the agricultural college, Hólar University, this brewery and pub is open at select times each week, namely Friday evenings. Hólar is a tiny community with little-over 100 residents and is most famous as the location where Iceland's first printing press was introduced in 1530. The settlement is also one of the country's oldest episcopal sees, providing Christian culture and education from 1106-1798. Such history is certainly enjoyable to consider while sipping back on the beer centre's most quality beverages.

272 BJÓRBÖÐIN BEER SPA

Ægisgata 31
Árskógssandi
621 Dalvík
Northeast Iceland
+354 414 2828
bjorbodin.is

The beer spa just outside of Dalvík takes relaxation to whole new heights. Working in collaboration with Kaldi Brewery, guests lie in a bathtub filled with warm beer, yeast, and hops for twenty-five minutes, allowing this miracle tonic to work wonders for their hair and skin. While the bathwater is undrinkable, beer taps beside each tub allows for constant top-ups while soaking. Outside, there is a sauna and two large hot tubs with fabulous views over nearby Hrísey Island. Their restaurant also offers a variety of gourmet dishes, including fish fried in beer batter and garlic roasted lobster.

273 ÖLVERK PIZZA & BREWERY

Breiðamörk 2
810 Hveragerði
South Iceland
+354 483 3030
olverk.is

Situated in Hveragerði, in the very heart of the Golden Circle sightseeing route, Ölverk Pizza & Brewery has been serving guests since spring 2017. Operating a two-barrel system, which capitalises on the towns' underground geothermal energy, Ölverk produces small-batch craft beers, which wonderfully complement their second speciality: premium wood-fired pizzas. Brewery tours last for up to 40 minutes, during which time guests are invited to sample four different Ölverk beers. The restaurant takes things one step further, serving over 36 different types of pizza.

274 RVK BREWING COMPANY

Skipholt 31
105 Reykjavík
Capital Region
+354 588 2337
rvkbrewing.com

On a tour of RVK Brewing Company's sleek facilities, guests are offered the opportunity to try golden nectar straight from the tanks, as well as taste six selected beers. The brewery is best known for their experimental recipes; for instance, a former Xmas beer was concocted using a real-life Christmas tree. There is also an offsite taproom at Snorrabraut where guests can enjoy the 16 craft beers on offer, as well as a spot of delicious BBQ.

FROST & FIRE HOTEL

SLEEP 🌙

Unwind at
HEARTSOME HOTELS

275 FROST & FIRE HOTEL

Hverhamar
810 Hveragerði
South Iceland
+354 483 4959
frostogfuni.is

Near Hveragerði's geothermal river, Varmá is a boutique hotel that offers its guests a lavish stay using subterranean energy. Riverside hot tubs, a relaxing sauna, and an outdoor pool are all among the hotel's luxurious amenities. Its sleek interior is decorated with captivating works by local artists, while outside, the steamy volcanic hillsides of Reykjadalur promise excellent hiking trails. Surrounding farmsteads provide the ingredients for the onsite Varmá Restaurant's à la carte dishes.

276 HÓTEL RANGÁ

Suðurlandsvegi
851 Hella
South Iceland
+354 487 5700
hotelranga.is

South Iceland's only four-star resort, Rangá is named after the nearby salmon river. The trickling feature can be seen running between Mount Hekla and Eyjafjallajökull volcano through the windows of any one of the hotel's 52 furnished rooms. Many come with spa baths, balconies and flatscreen televisions, though the real luxuries are found downstairs with the hotel's own cognac office and two sophisticated bars. In case this wasn't enough, Hótel Rangá also operates an advanced planetarium, regarded as one of the most impressive stargazing and Northern Lights facilities in Iceland.

277 FISHERMAN HÓTEL WESTFJORDS

Aðalgata 14-16
430 Suðureyri
Westfjords
+354 450 9000
fisherman.is

As its name suggests, this hotel in Suðureyri is all about showcasing Iceland's fishing heritage. The Fisherman Hótel offers not only delicious unprocessed dishes through its restaurant and small shop but also the Seafood Trail, a gourmet tour of the town led by a local food fanatic. The hotel itself has 19 rooms, some suited for travelling couples, others for the entire family, but all of which are perfect for seafood aficionados.

278 HÓTEL GLYMUR

Hvalfirði
301 Akranes
West Iceland
+354 430 3100
hotelglymur.is

Located 45 minutes from the capital on the northern end of Hvalfjörður, Hótel Glymur is another excellent choice for travellers looking to experience the very best of Iceland's western regions. There are 22 rooms in total, each with Italian leather furniture and marvellous views over the fjords and mountains. There are also two luxury suites, complete with alleviating massage-baths (perfect after a hard day travelling), and six themed villas with their own hot tubs and verandas.

279 FOSSHÓTEL GLACIER LAGOON

Hnappavellir
785 Öræfi
South Iceland
+354 514 8300
islandshotel.is

Nestled conveniently between the majestic nature reserve Skaftafell and Jökulsárlón glacier lagoon, this luxury 125-room hotel is an excellent accommodation choice for those who'll settle for nothing less than true immersion in nature. Fosshótel Glacier Lagoon is positioned directly beneath Iceland's highest peak, Hvannadalshnúkur (2110 m), and its restaurant offers cuisine equally dramatic, with an emphasis on creative dishes like creamy langoustine soup, smoked lamb carpaccio, and coffee-vanilla cured salmon.

280 HRAUNSNEF COUNTRY HOTEL

Hraunsnef
311 Borgarnes
West Iceland
+354 435 0111
hraunsnef.is

The comfortable and relaxed lodgings that comprise Hraunsnef Country Hotel include 15 cosy rooms with ensuite bathrooms, two smaller cottages, and one larger cottage able to accommodate up to five guests. There are also two bubbling hot pools, free to use night and day, and an outdoor fireplace, marking a lovely spot to chill out and socialise with family and friends. Don't be surprised if your party is interrupted by a four-legged intruder, however; cows, sheeps and goats happily roam the grounds.

Stay cosy in **COTTAGES** *and* **GUESTHOUSES**

281 HJARÐARBÓL COTTAGES

Hjarðarból
816 Þorlákshöfn
South Iceland
+354 567 0045
hjardarbol.is

Hjarðarból is a congenial and straightforward homestead located between Hveragerði and Selfoss. True to their mid-20th-century roots, these two cottages offer both national authenticity and unpretentious comfort. Guests can expect a generous breakfast buffet, followed by a spot of bathing in the outdoor hot pools, marking the perfect way to begin a day's sightseeing in South Iceland. Not only are the Golden Circle attractions found close by, but guests would do well to explore the greenhouses and steaming hot springs of Hveragerði.

282 SÖÐULSHOLT HORSE FARM & COTTAGES

Söðulsholt
311 Borgarnes
West Iceland
+354 895 5464
cottages.sodulsholt.is

Söðulsholt was a working farm until 1936, after which it became a parsonage, remaining so until 1994. Four years later, the land (covering nearly 118 hectares) was purchased by Einar Ólafsson, who dedicated himself to turning it into a horse breeding farm and centre for reforestation efforts. Only 31 kilometres from Borgarnes town, guests to these cottages are encouraged to take part in a short horseback riding tour or try their hands at salmon fishing in the nearby river.

283 ESJAN BUSES

Skrauthólar 4
162 Kjalarnes
Capital Region

At first glance, one might assume the Esjan Buses to be part of some long-disused scrapyard, but in fact, they make up one of Iceland's most unique renovated accommodations. The buses sit beneath the ridges of the tabletop mountain Esja, in the remote Kjalarnes district of Reykjavík. Each of the converted buses come complete with a seating/sleeping area and kitchenette, with shared bathrooms also found on-site.

284 KALASTAÐIR COTTAGES

Route 47
301 Akranes
West Iceland
+354 663 2712
(Thorvaldur)
+354 840 1225
(Brynja)
kalastadir.com

Built on the shoreline of a stunning waterbody, Kalastaðir Cottages make for picturesque accommodation. They are flawlessly situated for those looking to explore West Iceland's most beloved points of interest. As three separate properties, two are able to cater up to 2-4 guests while the larger can accommodate 6. All cottages have their own terrace, complete with BBQ facilities and a private hot tub. The owners also happen to have a great reputation as friendly folk eager to dish out some locals'knowledge.

285 DÆLI GUESTHOUSE

Dæli
531 Hvammstangi
Northwest Iceland
+354 451 2566
daeli.is

Dæli is a family-run guesthouse located in openly rural surroundings. Visitors can choose to stay in one of six small cabins, a luxury cottage or one of the 16 guesthouse bedrooms. The adjoined restaurant specialises in such traditional Icelandic dishes as salmon and lamb, though vegetarian options are also available. A nearby attraction is the massive rock stack Hvítserkur. This peculiar formation's name translates to 'White Shirt' because of the white bird droppings that permanently rest atop it.

286 ÁLFASTEINN COUNTRY HOME

Pjodolfshagi 25
851 Hella
South Iceland
+354 772 8304
icelandmagic.is

Open year-round, guests will share this quaint guesthouse with longtime resident Ágúst Rúnarsson, director of Iceland Magic Travel, who boasts over 40 years as a local guide. Not only does he cook the dinners throughout your stay, but also hosts sightseeing, hiking and horse riding tours of the nearby area. A holiday here is sure to have you experience Icelandic hospitality firsthand.

287 THE VIKING LODGE

Arnarbæli
801 Selfoss
South Iceland
vikinglodge.
heimaleiga.is

From its name alone, one might expect a traditional longhouse, or perhaps a turf-roof cabin set out amidst the forests of South Iceland. In fact, the four-bedroom Viking Lodge in Selfoss is incredibly contemporary, with polished interior decor, free Wi-Fi and a large flatscreen television. The patio offers a riverside view, and those spending their evenings in the bubbling hot tub might be privy to a Northern Lights display overhead.

Keep outdoors at cool

CAMPSITES

288 PATREKSFJÖRÐUR CAMPING GROUND

Aðalstræti 107
450 Patreksfjörður
Westfjords
+354 456 1515
westfjords.is

Camping near Patreksfjörður town means you've chosen to see Icelandic nature at its most raw; this is a given considering the campsite is wedged between a small river and a mountain. Patreksfjörður town offers only modest retail and dining opportunities, but its swimming pool is famed for having one of the best viewpoints in the entire country.

289 MOSSKÓGAR CAMPING

Dalsgarðsafleggjari
270 Mosfellsbær
Capital Region
+354 663 6173

Only a short drive from Reykjavík, Mosskógar Camping is a brilliant option for travellers seeking to experience the ruggedness of nature while also keeping close to the comfort and amenities of the city. With a laidback vibe, this campsite comes highly praised for allowing privacy among its guests. Outdoor showers and a large greenhouse, suitable for sleeping during rainy nights, count among the amenities. The surrounding area is picturesque and dense with tree cover, offering several scenic hiking trails closeby to Mosfellsbær town.

290 SKAGASTRÖND CAMPSITE

By Bogabraut road
545 Skagaströnd
Northwest Iceland
+354 776 0040
tjalda.is

Sheltered on both sides by the Hólaberg cliffs, Skagaströnd campsite is built around a small turf mound that once served as the foundation for an old farmstead. Today, there is a service house that allows guests to cater for themselves and do much-needed laundry. It's also the only spot to pick up information pamphlets on nearby walking trails, including those ascending the domineering Spákonufell (Fortune Teller's Mountain).

291 CAMP EGILSSTAÐIR

Kaupvangur 17
700 Egilsstaðir
East Iceland
+354 470 0750
campegilsstadir.is

A stone's throw from Egilsstaðir's shops and restaurants, this campsite is open throughout the year. There is 24/7 access to toilets, showers and laundry, free Wi-Fi and bicycle rentals. A stay here means you will likely be visiting such astounding eastern attractions as Selskógur Forest and Hengifoss waterfall.

292 HLÍÐ CAMPGROUND

Hraunbrún
660 Mývatn
Northeast Iceland
+354 464 4103
myvatn
accommodation.is

Hlíð Campground sits on the shores of Lake Mývatn, making it the ideal accommodation for campers looking to explore the many diverse attractions of Iceland's Northeast. Laundry service and warm showers are available free of charge for all guests, as well as furnished trailers and electricity access. With striking views over the lake and adjacent lava field, Hlíð campground is only a five-minute walk from a supermarket and tourist information office.

Rest at happening **HOSTELS**

293 **GALAXY POD HOSTEL**

Laugavegur 172
105 Reykjavík
Capital Region
+354 511 0505
galaxypodhostel.is

While much of Iceland still feels antiquated, Reykjavík's Galaxy Pod Hostel strives to impress with its futuristic aesthetic. Not unlike the iconic Japanese capsule hotels, guests will be designated their very own pod as a sleeping quarters, complete with a private TV screen, lockers and a safe. Galaxy Pod Hostel also offers a Virtual Reality room, a Scandinavian-style lounge bar, free Wi-Fi and a freshly stocked self-serving kitchen. If you're looking for budget accommodation with a real twist, look no further than here.

294 **BAKKI APARTMENTS & HOSTEL**

Eyrargata 51-53
820 Eyrarbakki
South Iceland
+354 788 8200
bakkihostel.is

Only two shops are found in Eyrarbakki town; there is Laugabúð, much the same as it was upon opening in 1900, and the local gas station and convenience store. Also nearby is Bakki Apartments & Hostel, particularly suited to those looking for privacy and solace. There are nine fully furnished studio apartments, and dormitories capable of accommodating up to 36 people, including 6-bed dorms for women only. The accommodation is built right on the seaside and is only a five-minute walk from the beloved Rauða Húsið restaurant. Eyrarbakki is another gateway town to the popular Golden Circle sightseeing route.

295 VIBRANT ICELAND HOSTEL

Kaplahraun 9-B
220 Hafnarfjörður
Capital Region
+354 419 2847
vibrant.is

Offering homebuilt bunk beds enclosed with curtains, Vibrant Iceland Hostel guarantees as much ease and comfort as is possible on the cheap. This includes fast-Wi-Fi, hotel-grade showers and a large shared kitchen where guests are free to dip into the fresh-bean coffee and tea. Vibrant Iceland Hostel is located in Hafnarfjörður, approximately eight kilometres from downtown Reykjavík, making it a good choice for return travellers looking for other places to stay in the Capital Region aside from the capital itself.

296 MIDGARD BASE CAMP

Dufþaksbraut 14
860 Hvolsvöllur
South Iceland
+354 578 3180
midgard.is

Modern, sophisticated and with all the necessary facilities on-site, Midgard Base Camp provides every luxury a traveller could ever desire while taking a respite from exploring South Iceland. Midgard Base Camp is particularly favoured for its thrilling 4x4 sightseeing excursions into the intrepid and often inaccessible Icelandic Highlands. The restaurant and bar also host live events throughout the year, as well as serving delectable dishes including prime lamb rib, smoked arctic char and pan-fried salmon.

297 THE BARN

Norðurfoss
871 Vík í Mýrdal
South Iceland
+354 779 1166
barnhostel.is

The seafront village, Vík, is a frequent sojourn along Iceland's south coast and is routinely utilised as a lunch stop by tour companies. Only seven kilometres away, The Barn hostel is considered one of the better accommodation options for those looking to extend their stay in Vík longer. Complimentary parking, double rooms and free Wi-Fi make staying overnight an easy affair. Well-rated by loved-up travelling couples, The Barn's sophisticated hostel bar is the best way to wind down after a long day exploring.

298 BLÁBJÖRG GUESTHOUSE

Gamla Frystihúsið
720 Borgarfjörður Eystri
East Iceland
+354 846 0085
blabjorg.is

Blábjörg Guesthouse is an all-round champion choice of accommodation, as it not only doubles as a restaurant (Frystiklefinn) but also a luxury day-spa (Musterið). The guesthouse is divided between luxury apartments for whole families and quaint cottages for smaller parties. Frystiklefinn restaurant offers international cuisine with an Icelandic twist, while the hot tubs of Musterið provide transcendent views over the mountains of the east.

Enjoy **OLD FARMHOUSE** stays

299 **OLD FARMHOUSE OF VEGAMÓT**
Vegamót
620 Dalvík
Northeast Iceland

Like all agricultural nations, Iceland has historically faced a mass exodus of people from the countryside to the city. Many farmsteads were left out of use until a recent wave of renovations saw them transformed into quality rural accommodation. One of the best examples of this is the Old Farmhouse Vegamót. This romantic red cottage is best suited for couples and families, with sleeping room for up to four people. Guests can expect free Wi-Fi and use of the outdoor hot tub. Next door to the cabin, one can find the amenities of Dalvík town, including a football field, pool and play area.

300 **ÓSEYRI FARMHOUSE**
Fjarðarbraut
East Iceland
+354 841 9308
oseyri755.com

Fifty-three kilometres from Egilsstaðir Airport is Óseyri Farmhouse, another brilliant option for travelling families, offering four bedrooms with two single beds apiece. Complete with a hot tub and BBQ facilities, the farmhouse terrace provides magnificent views of both the ocean and nearby mountains. The owners have recently taken to planting trees in the area as part of greater reforestation efforts across Iceland, so guests are asked to tread carefully around the property.

301 LANGAVATN GUESTHOUSE

Kísilvegur Road 87
Langavatn
641 Húsavík
Northeast Iceland
+354 852 8222
langavatn.com

Sat directly between the whale watching capital Húsavík and the natural splendour of Lake Mývatn, Langavatn Guesthouse is an excellent option for travellers looking to immerse themselves in the spectacle of Iceland's northern landscapes. The property is managed by a family who has lived and worked on the farm since 1848. To this day, Langavatn is still a working farm and home to over 300 sheep. A scrumptious breakfast is served each morning in the guesthouse restaurant.

302 STÓRA-ÁSGEIRSÁ FARM STAY

Stóra Ásgeirsá
531 Hvammstangi
Northwest Iceland
+354 866 4954
asgeirsa.com

Stóra-Ásgeirsá offers far more than your run-of-the-mill lodgings and is particularly suited for visitors looking to get their hands dirty. Guests are invited to help out with the farm work, providing firsthand knowledge as to how modern agriculture operates in Iceland. This includes help taking care of the animals, and any other task necessary for daily operations. During the summer, it is possible to rent horses directly from the farm, allowing guests to ride through the countless Saga sites dotted around the green lushness of Víðidalur Valley.

ÞJÓRSÁ

INDEX

COLOPHON

EDITING *and* COMPOSING – Michael Chapman – @mikeywchapman

GRAPHIC DESIGN – Joke Gossé and doublebill.design

PHOTOGRAPHY – Ívar Eyþórsson – @ivareythorsson

ADDITIONAL PHOTOGRAPHY – p.110: Arnar Tomasson

COVER IMAGE – Landmannalaugar hills (secret 63)

The addresses in this book have been selected after thorough independent
research by the author, in collaboration with Luster Publishing. The selection
is solely based on personal evaluation of the business by the author. Nothing
in this book was published in exchange for payment or benefits of any kind.

D/2022/12.005/8
ISBN 978 94 6058 2653
NUR 510, 512

© 2022 Luster Publishing, Antwerp
First edition, February 2022
lusterpublishing.com – THE500HIDDENSECRETS.COM
info@lusterpublishing.com

Printed in Italy by Printer Trento.